Back to the Future of the Roman Catholic Church

Back to the Future of the Roman Catholic Church

Theological and Ecclesiastical Perspectives on a Religious Institution at the Edge of Its Survival into the Twenty-First Century

Carmen J. Calvanese

Foreword by
Geffrey B. Kelly

WIPF & STOCK · Eugene, Oregon

BACK TO THE FUTURE OF THE ROMAN CATHOLIC CHURCH
Theological and Ecclesiastical Perspectives on a Religious Institution at the Edge of Its Survival into the Twenty-First Century

Copyright © 2014 Carmen J. Calvanese. All rights reserved. Except for brief quotations in critical publications or reviews, no part of this book may be reproduced in any manner without prior written permission from the publisher. Write: Permissions, Wipf and Stock Publishers, 199 W. 8th Ave., Suite 3, Eugene, OR 97401.

Scripture texts in this work are taken from the New American Bible, revised edition © 2010, 1991, 1986, 1970 Confraternity of Christian Doctrine, Washington, D.C. and are used by permission of the copyright owner. All Rights Reserved.

Wipf & Stock
An imprint of Wipf and Stock Publishers
199 W. 8th Ave., Suite 3
Eugene, OR 97401

www.wipfandstock.com

ISBN 13: 978-1-62564-091-8

Manufactured in the U.S.A.   10/23/2014

Contents

Foreword by Geffrey B. Kelly | vii

Preface | xiii

1 A Church in Crisis | 1
    Decreased Attendance at Sunday Mass | 2
    Numerous Parish Closings | 5
    Lack of Vocations to the Priesthood | 8
    Embarrassment and Cost of the Pedophile Clerics | 9
    Inability to Accept Dissent | 12
    Conclusion | 14

2 Shades of Modernity | 18
    Proposals for Change | 19
    Glimpse of the Future | 27
    Rahner's Concept of the Future | 30
    Return of the Faithful | 33
    Is There a Place for Women in the Priesthood? | 36
    Women Priests Today | 45

Contents

3 Church Ministry to the Poor: A Beacon of Hope for the Future Church | 48

   Portrait of Poverty in the Context of Church Credibility | 54

   Those Who Live the Message of Hope for the Church of the Poor: The Example of Dorothy Day | 61

   The Example of Archbishop Oscar Romero | 63

   The Example of Reinhold Niebuhr | 67

   The Need for Challenge in the Church | 71

4 Obstacles in the Ecumenical Movement | 76

   Hope for the Future, Obstacles to the Present | 76

   Ecumenical Theology of the Future: Toward Church Credibility as a Moral Force for Good | 88

   The Ecumenical Movement Today: The Church's Hope for a More Credible and Attractive Future | 90

   Conclusion | 97

5 The Possible and the Necessary in the Church's Future | 100

   A Community of Sisters and Brothers | 103

   Call for a Second Reformation | 107

6 Concluding Remarks | 114

Bibliography | 123

Foreword

FROM NEARLY EVERY SOCIOLOGICALLY based statistical analysis the Roman Catholic Church in the United States and throughout its international ministries has deteriorated to the point that its standing as an attractive moral and spiritual force for peace and justice in this troubled world has apparently been lost to the point that its very survival as a church is threatened. For those who continue to puzzle over what has happened to this church where once as believing Catholics they had derived their spiritual nourishment and were inspired to exemplary moral behavior by the church's pastoral leadership, this book by theologian Carmen J. Calvanese could not be more timely. Calvanese has meticulously investigated the various wide-ranging problems that plunged the Catholic Church into those devastating crises that, in turn, have eroded the Church's long-vaunted moral relevance and stymied its attractiveness to peoples still hungering for that viable spiritual community that, as faithful and faith-filled members, they had once enjoyed.

The problem Calvanese faces in charting the problems and the possible steps toward a future restoration of Church credibility has been admittedly compounded by the Church's reticence to admit that a crisis even existed in the first place and by the Church's seeming inability to accept criticisms and dissenting opinions aimed at renewing the Church or effecting several of the needed changes that Calvanese has focused on. Calvanese confronts the grim reality that, in nearly every church parish, attendance has plunged to staggering depths, particularly among young people at the secondary school and college levels. This troubling statistic is itself made

Foreword

more complex by its disturbing link to the Church's having also lost its appeal to potential candidates for ministry, a *condicio sine qua non* for Church renewal or even its survival. Calvanese takes his readers on an investigative journey to establish the data for his analyses of these church crises. He surveys the many reasons for the decrease in attendance at Sunday worship services, particularly among young people. He points out that this became a reality so frightening from an economic "supply and demand" viewpoint that several dioceses, under the leadership of financially astute bishops and archbishops, have seen themselves compelled to mandate parish closings, even among parishes still popular, though sparsely attended by an increasing elderly set of believers. These economically sound moves have resulted in angering parishioners forced to seek services elsewhere.

Calvanese uses his statistical data to turn his attention to the concomitant problem, namely, the lack of vocations to the priesthood. This drain on the personnel involved in parish ministry has forced upon church leaders the realization that parishes can no longer be served by sufficient priests on a regular basis. Calvanese not only documents the reasons for this decline in candidates for church ministry but he uses his data to critically question the Church's reluctance to move away from its rigid requirement for celibacy on the part of potentially qualified male candidates to the priesthood. Doing away with that requirement could, he points out, open the doors for a restoration to priestly status of several priests who have left the ministry to marry and thereby lost their faculties to function as priests. Calvanese argues further that lifting this discipline—a requirement to be celibate unrelated to Jesus' own followers in the early church—would eliminate a major obstacle to potential candidates who would otherwise apply to enter the priestly ministry. Calvanese is aware of the Church's long-standing reluctance to change its requirement of priestly celibacy. At the same time, in the light of the shortage of priests and the phenomenon of the parish closings, he directs his most critical objections to the discipline at the stubborn, unreasonable insistence on clerical celibacy by present-day Church hierarchs. In a second chapter he raises the possibility of admitting women to the priesthood, though he admits that, given present Church's "definitive" documents, such a possibility can only be a future step that can only be hoped for.

At this juncture in his explorations of the reasons that are most decisive in explaining the extreme depth to which several dioceses of the Roman Catholic Church had sunk is Calvanese's extensive analysis of the embarrassing, criminal behavior of the pedophile priests. He links the unraveling of this scandalous behavior to the costs that have arisen from the lawsuits directly related to and emanating from the cover-up tactics of misguided Church leaders who either kept the priests' sexual abuse of innocent children a secret while denying compensation to the children (many grown to adulthood with related psychological problems), or had conspired in the interests of secrecy to transfer the pedophile priests to other assignments where they only continued their infamous behavior. He associates the behavior of the dioceses that sheltered the pedophile priests with their having been hit hard by lawsuits and costs so severe that some dioceses had been forced into bankruptcy. Calvanese's documentation of this widespread abuse on the part of Church leaders and dioceses reveals the extent to which the scandals have damaged the moral fiber and trustworthy authority of the Catholic Church. The fact that so many dioceses and even one prominent religious order had to sell church property, file for bankruptcy, and see their cash reserves nearly obliterated constitutes, in Calvanese's judgment from this evidence, a crisis, both economic and spiritual, that will haunt Church credibility for years to come.

Related to the Church's self-serving attempt to cover up the scandalous criminality of the pedophile priests is, as Calvanese points out in a concluding segment of his analysis of the "Church in crisis," an unintended result of Church's apparent inability to accept dissent and criticism. He detects this fault as specific to those ultra-conservative Church leaders who mistakenly hold onto the notion that dissent, criticism, or modification in current Church practice will only hinder or smother the ideal of Church unity. They seem mired in the fear that the Church would split into several factions if dissenting opinions about Church governance, policies, and mandates were questioned. Calvanese sees in this attitude the real issue of the ultra-conservatives' myopic presumption that any criticism or dissent will result only in their loss of control and power over the faithful. The irony, as Calvanese notes, is that their attitude has the unwelcomed and unintended effect of causing their loss of moral credibility, and a rapid diminution of their authoritarian power over the faithful. Their failure to rationally consider valid points of dissent or accept well-grounded criticism aimed at improving Church life has only branded their leadership of the Catholic Church as too often out of touch with common sense or unconcerned with the well-being of the faithful whom they have been commissioned to lead.

Foreword

Calvanese's conclusions on the need for the Church to exercise authority in a manner that is faithful to the original vision for a church community by none other than Jesus Christ himself leads Calvanese to devote several sections of his book to attempts aimed at the restoration of Church credibility for the future that, given the foundational inspiration of Jesus Christ, he entitles a "Back to the Future." Calvanese explores several refreshing and exciting new ways in which the Church can rebuild its moral credibility and spiritual strength to become a Christ-centered church once again. To achieve this aim he develops a threefold program. In a first set of creative suggestions to restore the moral and spiritual credibility of the Roman Catholic Church at once faithful to the foundational inspiration of Jesus Christ, Calvanese returns to the works of creative theologians whose writings had become the grist of the major reforms of Vatican Council II. Among these, he emphasizes the innovative work of Karl Rahner, who played a major role in nearly every document that had been approved at the council and beyond. Taking a cue from Rahner's incisive essay warning the Catholic Church "not to stifle the inspiration of the Holy Spirit," Calvanese studies texts that had opened new pathways into being Church for the modern era, such as the work of liberation theologians, epitomized by Jon Sobrino, Leonardo Boff, and Gustavo Gutiérrez, all of whom had run into difficulty with conservative Church authorities but whose efforts succeeded in helping the Church become a "beacon of hope for the future." Here too Calvanese includes the insights of activists known for their devotion to the poor, so central to the concerns of a Church faithful to the teachings and example of Jesus Christ. He shows that the inspiration of significant Catholic leaders like Dorothy Day and Archbishop Oscar Romero can offer both light and influence on Church leaders and help to raise up activists who live the gospel message and represent the future of a Church renewed and reborn in its dedication to become a credible and attractive presence of Jesus Christ for the future.

Calvanese continues his "rebuilding" the moral credibility of the Roman Church through analyses of texts that have portended hopes for the kind of Church renewal that will enhance not merely the Church's image as a moral force for a troubled world but as a Church even more capable of bringing hope and relief to those still suffering from oppression, relief and greater freedom in pockets of human misery around the world. Calvanese integrates into his efforts at Church reform and renewal the innovative writings of creative theologians like Johann Baptist Metz in his "political

Foreword

theology" and his insistence for a continued Church relevance in the areas where faith and social justice inevitably intersect. Calvanese likewise refers to the recent work of Dominican theologian Timothy Radcliffe, whose own suggestions to effect a renewed Church as a force for a meaningful Christlike presence in a world in need of the sustenance that a revitalized Catholic Church could offer the world. Above all, Calvanese charts a path toward Church renewal not unlike Karl Rahner's own innovative book *The Shape of the Church to Come*, as well as the ecclesiology of the recently deceased Dominican scholar Edward Schillebeeckx, whose volumes defining the nature of the Church include convincing analyses of the Church as a community always formed and reformed in the human image of Jesus Christ in order for the Catholic Church to become as it always should have been, a light to the developed and developing world.

Finally, this book by Calvanese is unique in the author's ability to investigate in detail not only the problems that confront the present Roman Catholic Church but also to explore in a compelling way the new pathways of change and the unending need to search out sources of creative renewal that together offer hope for the present and courage to face the unknown future of the Church eager to remain in the power of the Holy Spirit of Jesus Christ. This books offers readers the many ways that a Church in crisis can, nonetheless, be enabled to rebuild its moral credibility and become an attractive and effective force for peace, justice, and reconciliation for the future. In the author's own title, the church must *return back to its origins* in the life and teachings of Jesus Christ to its best *future* as a Church continuing to represent Jesus Christ to the Christian world of every denomination and become a light of hope for the non-Christian world.

Geffrey B. Kelly, PHD, LLD

Professor of Systematic Theology
La Salle University
Philadelphia, PA

Preface

GROWING UP IN THE Catholic school system, I developed a deep and abiding respect for the Roman Catholic Church, its priests, bishops, and even the sitting pope. Even as far back as sixth grade, I can remember Sister Marcella, a dedicated nun in the Saint Joseph's congregation, tell the class that if we were walking down the street and saw a priest and an angel at the same time, we should always greet the priest first, because priests were higher than angels in the sight of God. Who were we to question such advice?

As the years flew by I grew into manhood and was better educated on the nature of the Catholic Church. It was then I came to the more mature realization that the leaders of the Church were merely human, and as such quite capable of making mistakes—some catastrophic, others egotistical, and some for no clearly identifiable reason. Many of those leaders seemed to live solely for experiencing the enhancement of their personal hierarchical authority and control. Others, I learned, were the antithesis of perfection I had once attributed. According to Tom Stella, the Church could at times be infected with "petty politics and dysfunctional people."

Today more than ever in its previous history, the Church seems to be in the throes of recurring crises. As we shall see in the following pages, there are many practical reasons for this quandary. The world seems to be in the midst of another "great awakening" that is taking on the character of a materialistic secularized society that is focused on sex, violence, greed, and the mindless pursuit of wealth and power. This secularization appears to have even made inroads into the various aspects of the Catholic Church itself. The more obvious evidence of this can be measured by the lack of

Preface

attendance at Sunday Mass, the critical shortage of priests, the closing of many parishes, a significant loss of vocations to the priesthood and religious life, the ongoing discrimination against women, the inability of leadership to accept reasonable dissent and practices that have been declared absolute by authoritarian decree, and the problems and inconsistencies in the Catholic Church's hesitant participation in the ecumenical movement. These problems have been compounded by actions on the part of some Church leaders to adequately care for and defend the poor and oppressed in areas of the world where systemic injustice has made ordinary people suffer from rampant denial of their human dignity and civil rights. Finally, the most recent stumbling block to Church respectability that has caused dishonor to the priestly ministry and degradation to contemporary Catholicity has been the onerous behavior and embarrassing cost of pedophile priests in the world, especially the United States.

This book's focus is the subject of these problems and concerns, and engages in the critical examination of the failure of the current Church leadership to adapt to a changing world. In order to gauge the causes of the Church's loss of credibility as a moral force and exemplar for people in every walk of society in the modern world, it will be necessary to explore the failure of leadership in the hierarchical structures of the Catholic Church, those who have displayed the inflexibility to come to terms with what the faithful parishioners and the present social reality demand. It appears from research that these very Church leaders have been clinging to nostalgia for the Church's former domination and glory. This book also examines how problems in the Church are related to the hierarchy's seeming unwillingness or inability to change, update, or modify doctrines, canons, and practices that, by their antiquated and at times irrelevant nature, have undermined the Church's credibility and attractiveness even to its own baptized faithful in recent years.

Further, I will attempt to bring to light many of the obstacles that presently exist in the Roman Catholic Church, impeding it from coping adequately with the unending challenge to become a Church more Christlike and morally credible, or in a celebrated phrase of Vatican Council II, an *ecclesia simper reformanda* (a Church always in the process of reforming itself). We contend here that it is time for the leadership to act and return to the Church's original roots as a witness to the teachings and continued presence of Jesus Christ. Our tentative conclusion will be that the Roman Catholic Church can and must return to the core of who it is called to be, as the people of God, followers of risen Savior. Only then can the Church

Preface

transcend itself and return "Back to Its Future" through the renewed fidelity to the gospel of Christ in today's secular world.

In a second phase, this book addresses the ways and means by which the Catholic Church can better inspire the faithful to fulfill their hopes in their Church and become themselves witnesses to the presence of none other than Jesus Christ among them. While the early chapters are focused on the crises that have caused deterioration in Church effectiveness and credibility as a witness to the presence of Christ, the ensuing chapters will offer an examination of just how the process of reform and restoration can be effected in many areas. In one of these areas, I will show how and why the Church is still admired for its dedication to the participation in the ecumenical movement in communion with other confessions in a healing of the original wounds that caused the reprehensible separation of the Christian churches. Today the same Catholic Church offers a significant promise for Christianity to be united in a more prophetic manner, as together they bear witness to the gospel values that should inspirit every society where Christian churches exist to promote justice and peace in the name of Jesus Christ.

In the first of these "restorative" chapters, I contend that the Church offers a reinforcement of a principal source of its present credibility, namely, its attractive service to the poor. It is here that I present the reasons why and how the Catholic Church became a Church of the poor and abused. This feature of Church life, more so than any pronounced respect for the hierarchy, stands as living evidence that the Church has never lost its original calling to be a Church of the impoverished in spirit dedicated to be the providential force that hungers and thirsts for justice. The Church witness as to Christianity's most appealing fidelity to the presence of Jesus' compassion for the poor abound in this chapter. It presents prophetic figures like Archbishop Oscar Romero, Dorothy Day, and liberation theologians like Gustavo Gutiérrez and Jon Sobrino, who have become the voices of the voiceless in areas of the world, where the poor are exploited, abused, and made to suffer injustice. These prophetic leaders exemplify the Church's hope for its future and the confidence that the faithful need in the Church to become once again by its service to the poor an attractive light of the world through its unstinting service to the poor, the weak, the vulnerable victims of heartless societies in today's world.

Following a chapter that addresses the importance of its participation in the ecumenical movement as a crucial factor in the Catholic Church's return to credibility and inspiration, I analyze what is "possible and necessary" for the Catholic Church to become a moral force capable of capturing the worldwide influence it once enjoyed and its attractiveness for potential followers of Jesus Christ to find in the Church a spiritual home. I draw on the creative insights of three theologians whose writings have exerted widespread influence on the manner in which the structures of the Catholic Church can be reshaped into a renewed Church, both in its internal life among the baptized faithful and in its outreach to serve the needy of the world through the grace of the Holy Spirit and in the freedom of Christians that Jesus Christ made possible through his gospel as exemplified in his life. The authors in question are Timothy Radcliffe, Karl Rahner, and Johann Baptist Metz.

First of these theologians is Timothy Radcliffe, former Superior General of the Dominican religious order, who has published a series of recent studies of the present Church that offer a renewal process similar to the fresh insights that Pope John XXIII made possible through Vatican Council II. Next, Jesuit theologian Karl Rahner, considered the most creative and influential theologian since Thomas Aquinas, has composed a clear and compelling analysis of "The Shape of the Church to Come." Rahner views the future of the Church that is "declericalized," with decreased emphasis on hierarchical control systems, its openness to dissent, its democratization in an emphasis on genuine community, its being a socio-political Church able to creatively dialogue with moral power with the secular powers of the day, and its role with how best to serve its faithful and the forces of the secular world so capable of the grossest injustice, such as that which bedeviled the world by the Nazis, or that which continues in areas of injustice and repression throughout the present-day world. Finally, I have focused on the writings of Johann Baptist Metz, whose "political theology" has particular application to one of the most attractive features of Roman Catholicism, namely, its involvement in the socio-political world as a voice for the rights of all peoples to a life of dignity and personal prosperity. Metz's theology opens an additional path to a restoration of Church credibility and attractiveness, namely, the Church's admirable advocacy of the right to life, whether by the victims of unnecessary abortions, those condemned to death in societies where the death penalty is still in vogue, and the more complex and troubling issue of being a "peace church" daring to preach peace in a world still torn apart by what seems to be endless wars.

In sum, these theological insights could be integrated into present-day Church life with effects of renewing and enabling it to experience a rebirth into the spirit of its origins as an exemplary example of the teachings of Jesus

Preface

Christ, with enhanced relevance and augmented attractiveness; for faithful Christians are eager to have their spiritual needs and desires fulfilled in the Catholic Church of today and tomorrow. In the following pages, therefore, I will attempt not only to analyze the crisis the Church faces today, but also to demonstrate the reasons why and how the Roman Catholic Church can become, once again, faithful in its service to people and its fidelity to the teachings and inspiring example of Christ Jesus.

For the fact that this study ever reached its present form I am indebted to the input and guidance from my teacher and mentor, Dr. Geffrey B. Kelly, from the Religion Department of La Salle University. I am likewise grateful to my friends and associates from the Liberal Arts Department at Manor College, and especially the instructor that encouraged me to "follow my bliss," Dr. Madeline Seltzer, who originally ignited the spark within to take this journey of study. And last, but certainly not the least, I profoundly acknowledge my deep affection and gratitude to my wife, Ellen, who is the love of my life and greatest inspiration. Ellen is my soul mate and the person who changed my life. No one would put up with me other than a person of great faith during my years of schooling and what seemed to be the days and nights of endless classes and study. I thank you ever so much.

1

A Church in Crisis

THIS FIRST CHAPTER EXPLORES the awareness in contemporary ecclesiology that, indeed, the Roman Catholic Church is in the midst of crisis. The obvious evidence that the Church is struggling can be ascertained in a number of differing ways: the decreased attendance at Sunday Mass, the numerous parish closings, the lack of vocations, the embarrassment and legal cost of pedophile clerics, the inability to accept reasonable dissent and criticism, and the current rigidity in the ecumenical movement that undermines opportunities for unity with other denominational confessions. This crisis could easily become a disaster waiting to implode from within, and can only be avoided by massive conversion of hearts, well-needed structural changes, and reasonable modification of present attitudes among the leaders of the Church. More conspicuously, a transformation will occur—which seems to have already begun in breakaway movements within the Catholic Church—where, through the power of the Holy Spirit, change and modernization will come from the grass roots of the faithful and spread upwards to the leaders at the top. This quiet revolution will eventually bring with it a new beginning for the Church in an age that will take it back to its origins of love, forgiveness, and understanding with compassion towards all. This potential new Church will center on the gospel word of Jesus Christ with loving care for all the faithful—saints and sinners alike.

Although the Church will never cease to exist, it is currently besieged with challenges and difficulties, most of which are the result of its own making. Today, more than ever, there is a need for a Christ-centered radicalism that is focused on the gospel in the praxis of the Church's catholicity. The challenge for a spiritual revolution is in the making. Its purpose will be centered in forgiveness, forbearance, and tolerance for dissent and developmental change. In other words, there needs to be a call for renewal within the Church that unites all Christians in mutual love and understanding through living the gospel of Christ. Yet, in spite of less than subtle warnings from within and without the Church, bonds of rigidity persist among its leaders. Contemporary theologians, like the prophets of old, caution the hierarchy on the need to address the call to reform and change its ways. Thus far, most warnings have gone unnoticed, ignoring Jesus' own advice to his followers to note "the signs of the time" (Matt 16:3). In the following segments, we will examine some of these present-day signs.

Decreased Attendance at Sunday Mass

In Europe, for example, where Christendom once flourished, attendance at Sunday Mass is in near shattering proportional decline. In every major city on the continent, attendance is down to unprecedented levels. In Italy, for instance, 97 percent of the population is Catholic, however, attendance at Sunday Mass has dropped to an average of 30 percent of the faithful, according to figures compiled by *Familia Cristiana*, a popular Catholic weekly magazine.[1] In major cities like Milan, Florence, and Rome attendance at Sunday Mass is no more than 15 percent of the Catholic populace.[2]

In France, moreover, 76 percent of the population is Catholic but attendance at Sunday Mass accounts for a mere 12 percent.[3] According to Georgetown University's Center for the Study of Global Christianity and Vatican Officials, "The percentage attending Sunday Mass has dropped to a low of 5 percent in most of France's major cities."[4] This statistic appears to be the trend in most of Western Europe. The magnificent cathedrals that were built in the earlier centuries on the sweat and coin of the faithful have turned into empty shrines that are more visited by tourists than used for Sunday worship.[5]

1. "Europe, the Collapse of the Catholic Church."
2. Ibid.
3. Ibid.
4. Ibid.
5. Ibid.

A Church in Crisis

In Germany, the Church has likewise suffered substantially on all fronts. From the 1960s, atheistic and militant college students blamed the establishment, particularly the Catholic Church, for its supportive involvement with the Nazi party. They denounced politicians and Church officials for their collaboration with the Hitler regime. Even at the celebratory Mass for Pope Benedict XVI, in his hometown of Traunstein, there were no more than seventy-five parishioners in attendance in a church that seats a thousand.[6] Winfried Roehmel, director of the press office for the Archdiocese of Munich, made the bold observation that about one third of the German population are nominally Catholic, but fewer than 13 percent attend Mass with any regularity.[7] Germany's Catholic Church has come to be known as a "creeping decay."[8]

In Ireland, too—a country that is well known for its strong attachment to the teachings and practices of the Catholic Church, where thirty years ago 91 percent of Catholics faithfully attended Sunday Mass—presently less than 50 percent now attend Mass barely once a month.[9] Amid the growth in Ireland that came with economic prosperity, few dispute the notion that "the edifice of Catholicism is in danger of a cracking along its foundation."[10]

In Spain the situation is not much better. An article entitled "Europe, the Collapse of the Catholic Church" notes that "the Church is still in the process of emerging from the shadow of its alliance with the fascist dictator, Francisco Franco, who came into power as a 'liberator' in the late 1930's and died in 1975."[11] However, in spite of its strong Catholic traditions, most Spaniards do not participate regularly in religious services. A study that was made in October of 2006 by the "Spanish Centre of Sociological Research shows that of the Spaniards who identify themselves as religious, 54 percent hardly ever, or never, go to church. Of these, 15 percent go to church some times during the year, 10 percent attend church occasionally or at least once a month, and 19 percent attend Sunday mass or multiple times per week. What is important to note about the Catholic Church of Spain is that those who identify themselves as Catholics ignore the Church's stance on issues such as premarital sex, sexual orientation, and contraception. It

6. Ibid.
7. Ibid.
8. Ibid.
9. Ibid.
10 Ibid.
11. Ibid.

seems that the Church has certainly lost a great deal of its influence and authoritative control in Spain.[12]

Poland also, once a solid bastion of Catholicism, has likewise seen a significant decrease in attendance at Sunday Mass. The Church as the sign of stability during the reign of Pope John Paul II is now seen as drifting amidst the absence of its papal hero.[13] Collectively, in Europe, given these statistics, scholars believe that the Catholic Church is on the verge of collapsing and losing its creditability as an influential and moral force in the world.[14]

Some national churches have looked to the Catholic Church for hope. However, even in the United States, one of the strongholds of Catholicism, though the numbers of Catholics that attend Sunday Mass are much higher on a percentage basis, these figures have significantly deteriorated since Vatican II. According to the Center for Applied Research in the Apostolate (CARA), attendance at Sunday Mass by Catholics in the United States remained fairly unchanged between 2000 and 2004.[15] Nonetheless, in a report released by the independent Catholic research agency based at Georgetown University, there has been a long-term decline in attendance.[16] In intervening polls, two reliable resources reported that only 39 percent of Catholics attended weekly Mass in February 2002, as opposed to 35 percent in May of that year.[17] Citing Gallup polls, the Center for Applied Research in the Apostolate reported that Sunday Mass attendance in a given week apparently peaked at 74 percent in 1957–58, then gradually declined to about 41 percent in 1997, then spiked briefly to a new peak of 52 percent in 2000 before falling back to a low of 40 percent in 2003.[18] From this, author John McCloskey has concluded that "The Catholic Church in the United States is in a state of profound transition."[19] Since before Vatican II, 75 percent of American Catholics attended Sunday Mass regularly, however, from 2004 to 2006 those numbers have declined by over half.[20] By 2008, the number

---

12. Wikipedia, "Roman Catholicism in Spain."
13. Ibid.
14. Ibid.
15. CARA, "Frequently Requested Catholic Church Statistics."
16. Ibid.
17. Ibid.
18. Ibid.
19. McCloskey, "State of the US Catholic Church."
20. Ibid.

of Catholics that attended Sunday Mass on an average had leveled off to 36 percent.[21]

In Latin America, for instance, where 43 percent of the world's Catholics reside, the problem is similar, to the point that less than half attend Sunday Mass.[22] Even Pope Benedict XVI's Brazilian visit in 2007 was disappointing. In the pontiff's closing open-air Mass in Aparecida, out of 400,000–500,000 worshippers expected to attend, approximately 150,000 participated.[23] To say that the Church's attractiveness has deteriorated as a result of the dwindling attendance at Sunday Mass is a gross understatement. If this trend continues, Sunday Mass as we know it may dwindle to near irrelevance as a *conditio sine qua non* as a mark of identity for belonging to the Catholic Church.

Numerous Parish Closings

The crisis in Church attendance has been compounded by the astounding number of parish closings in the United States. Often these closing have been the result of the Catholic Church's direct response to the lack of parishioners and priests. In some other cases, closings are related to aging communities where younger Catholic families have moved to suburbia, into newer and more modern neighborhoods. This has generally been the rule in the United States, where the demographics seem to shift every thirty to forty years. Nevertheless, since Vatican II there has been a steady increase in the number of parish closings. The problem appears especially acute in older Catholic centers, where the movement of Catholics to the suburbs and a steady decrease of priests are two of the main reasons for closing parishes. Catholics in Albany, New York, for example, were recently notified by the bishop to expect the loss of up to 20 percent of the parishes in the diocese. This amounted to more than thirty sites.[24] In Camden, New Jersey, a diocese that stretches from the Delaware River to the shores of the Atlantic Ocean, Bishop Joseph A. Galante recently announced that he is making substantial cuts in the number of parishes. Within a two-year period his goal is to close 58 of 124 parishes, a significant cut for what the Apostle Peter has called the "people of God" (1 Pet 2:9–10). During the last

---

21. CARA, "Frequently Requested Catholic Church Statistics."
22 23 Stammer, "Attendance Is a Concern for Church."
23 24 Associated Press, "Pope Urges Latin American Bishops."
24. Roberts, "Parish Closing Traumas Spread."

15 years, 700 parishes have been closed in the northern and eastern region of the United States.[25] The Center for Applied Research of the Apostolate at Georgetown University has determined that because of realignments and mergers, presently there are 18,479 active parishes in the US, while in 1995 there were 19,331—a decline of more than 852 parishes over 14 years.[26]

For the Church, parish closings usually bring frustration to the community. The laity feels that bishops are diminishing their spiritual security and source of bonding as Catholics, values that provide a sense of communion. These closings often result in a great loss for the Church as a whole. Occasionally, those who become emotionally upset and feel the pain of rejection when their parish church is closed stage sit-ins and take control of church buildings, with expectation of reversals from diocesan bishops. In retaliation, bishops have been known to summon police and have disillusioned Catholics evicted from the premises. Such actions conjure feelings of disappointment and bitterness toward the Church, and often the faithful stray to other more friendly confessions. One might ask: is this the way to build up the "body of Christ" (1 Cor 12:13) and create a community of the faithful?

Marti Jewell, director of Emerging Models of Pastoral Leadership (EMPL), believes that beyond grieving parishioners and beleaguered priests there lies the question of lay ministry. However, bishops that do not prefer the lay option are using priest shortages as a reason to close and consolidate healthy parishes that could easily survive with the help of a "parish life coordinator."[27] Jewell offers a solution to the dilemma and makes the observation that restructuring of parishes is inevitable and can happen in two ways: first, "the model of a priest pastoring multiple parishes," and second, the use of "parish life coordinators operated by laypeople that are appointed by bishops to operate parishes in significant areas with the exception of sacramental ministries."[28]

The difficulty encountered in the first instance is the lack of support from bishops, not only in terms of personal contact with parish leadership, but pastoral also in the task of presenting clear visions for the future of the affected communities in light of broader diocesan plans.[29]

---

25. Kandra, "Camden Announces Largest Closing."
26. Roberts, "Parish Closing Traumas Spread."
27. Ibid.
28. Ibid.
29. CPPCD and NFPC, *Multiple Parish Pastoring*, 28.

In the daily operation of pastoring multiple parishes, the complexities include lack of quality time afforded to each community, the distance between the parishes, and the deficiency of financial resources to operate the ministry efficiently.[30] Additionally, priests must have a clear mandate for the liturgy and sacramental life of the community.[31] In the second instance, there needs to be openness to the 1983 Code of Canon Law, 517.2, which states:

> If the diocesan bishop should decide that due to the death of a priest, a participation in the exercise of the pastoral care of a parish is to be entrusted to a deacon or some other person, who is not a priest or to a community of persons; he is to appoint some priest endowed with the powers and faculties of a pastor to supervise the pastoral care.[32]

This new law opened the door to the use of Parish Life Coordinators (PLC) in those parishes that are not under the pastoral direction of a priest. Their duties include sacramental preparation, the operation of a parish, and liturgical ministry during Mass. Their main function, however, is meeting with parish councils and maintaining the budget and financial well-being of the community. Deacon Parish Life Coordinators usually maintain the sacramental functions; they spend much of their time preparing and giving homilies, presiding at baptisms, and officiating funerals, Sunday celebrations, and the prayer service for the sick. In most instances, deacon Parish Life Coordinator's receive a stipend for their services.[33] In any event, the bishop has the power to appoint a priest to manage and organize multiple parishes. He may even appoint a Parish Life Coordinator to operate a parish rather than close it, especially if there is support from the community and great desire from the laity not to close a parish.

In most instances, when bishops close single or multiple parishes such actions can often bring out the worst in the laity, especially in light of recent sex abuse scandals and the billions of dollars it has cost the Church in settlements and legal fees. It is emotionally unsettling for parishioners to think that the Church has paid unbelievable sums to deserving victims but now must close their parish for economic reasons. This crisis will not easily go away. An increase in the number of candidates for the priesthood could

---

30. Ibid., 26.
31. Ibid., 26.
32. Ibid., 4.
33. Ibid., 4.

seemly provide an antidote for this problem. But even here major problems exist, which will be addressed in the next segment.

Lack of Vocations to the Priesthood

In terms of the number of priests called to serve the Church, the priesthood itself appears in near collapse. In many ways the United States mirrors the lack of vocations and the declining number of priests in the countries of Europe.[34] The downward spiral of available priests seems indicative of the Church itself. For example, in 1965, at the end of Vatican Council II, there were 58,000 priests in the United States; presently there are approximately 41,000. If this trend continues—and there is no reason to believe that it will not— by the year 2020 there will be 31,000 ministering priests in America, and more than half will be over the age of 70.[35] This decline is a very serious challenge for the Catholic Church.

Ordinations have fallen to alarming rates. In 1965, 994 seminarians were ordained to the priesthood in America; in 2008, a mere 480.[36] Even in the religious communities the number of men and women taking vows has deteriorated to unbelievable levels in the US. Moreover, in 1965 there were 22,707 religious order priests, while at present there are 14,137, and most of the men are retired or approaching retirement age. In addition to the decline in priests, the religious brothers too have significant losses: in 1965 there were 12,271 brothers in the United States; presently there are a total of 5,451.[37] The most astonishing statistic, though, pertains to religious women: in 1965 there were 179,954 women committed to serve in religious congregations; in 2005 that number fell to 86,634, and presently there are more women over the age of 90 than there are under the age of 30.[38] In the religious communities too the number of men joining the houses of formation of Jesuits and Christian Brothers has declined by the alarming rate of 90–99 percent.[39] For the Catholic Church of America, as well as Europe, there are few signs of revival in this area of ministry.[40] These statics are

34. McCloskey, "State of the US Catholic Church."
35. Ibid.
36. Ibid.
37. Ibid.
38. Ibid.
39. Ibid.
40. Ibid.

overwhelmingly negative and offer grave concern for the future health of the Church in both America and Europe.

Embarrassment and Cost of the Pedophile Clerics

The present-day embarrassment and cost of pedophile priests has been devastating to the moral credibility of the Catholic Church. The unthinkable has become the reality. Deviate pedophile priests sexually abused innocent children and have become headlines in America and indeed the civilized world for the longest time. This well-kept secret has for years been a humiliation for the leadership of the Church and continues to be so to this very day. When allegations of abuse by pedophile priests appeared in the media, they brought with them a great sense of mistrust, disappointment, and skepticism to Catholics. These crimes against unsuspecting children were not exclusive to the United States; they have also surfaced in Western Europe, especially in Ireland.

For example, in Ireland the story unfolded in Galway in 1992 with news that Bishop Casey had an affair in 1974 with an American divorcee. During that period he fathered a child and attempted to hush the story by bribing the mother with diocesan funds. A short time later the incident hit the front page of the *Sunday Independent*, one of Ireland's largest newspapers.[41] Soon thereafter Mary Kenny recounted the story:

> People were flabbergasted, appalled and disbelieving; Catholic commentators went back over two hundred years to look for a parallel. Some even expressed the view that this was such an aberration, such a one-of a kind, that it was the unique exception, which proved the rule that Irish Catholic clergy were generally people of high probity, decency, and honor.[42]

From that time forward it all seemed downhill for the Catholic Church of Ireland. Scandals surfaced one after another. It was like turning on a light in a darkened room. Shame and embarrassment touched every order of priests, and included nuns and brothers alike. It was an ugly period in Irish Catholic history, and no doubt many Irish lost their love, respect, and trust for the Church.

---

41. Kenny, *Goodbye to Catholic Ireland*, 204.
42. Ibid., 309.

But the scandals were not exclusively Irish. In the United States too an estimated 4 percent of Catholic priests were accused of having engaged in pedophilic acts against children.[43] The John Jay Report, commissioned by the US Conference of Catholic Bishops, compiled a survey that was based on information that surfaced from secret diocesan files. In these documents there contained the names of priests that were accused of sexual abuse alongside the names of their victims. The information was heavily censored, so the researchers were not able to know who was involved. The report found accusations against 4,392 priests in the US, equaling to about 4 percent of all priests between the years of 1950 and 2002.[44] Without a doubt, these figures were appalling. American Catholics, like the Irish, were heartbroken, dismayed, and seriously lacked confidence in Church leadership when the news went public. As a result, many began to ask whether anyone could now trust the hierarchy because of the widespread abuses that were secretly covered up by at least one third of the American Catholic bishops.[45]

Most notable among the American hierarchy who were accused of transferring pedophiles from one assignment to another was Cardinal Bernard F. Law of Boston. After the media exposed the sexual abuses by the clergy and authorities were alerted, he resigned in disgrace. Conveniently, the cardinal was transferred to the safety of the Vatican and given an honorary position.[46] In the opposite end of the country, Cardinal Roger M. Mahony of Los Angeles was also accused of transferring pedophile priests. Former priest Oliver O'Grady, an admitted pedophile whose predatory activity went on in California for twenty years, has claimed that Mahony knew what he (O'Grady) was doing and elected to move him from one assignment to another. When O'Grady was finally caught by the authorities, he served seven years in prison on four counts of "lewd and lascivious acts" with two preteen brothers. Cardinal Mahony denied such allegations, but O'Grady claims he met with the cardinal and discussed his weakness in a face-to-face meeting.[47] These allegations led the faithful to wonder who is guilty of the greater sin: the pedophile priests, or those in charge that sanctioned their transfers with knowledge of these heinous crimes? It is

---

43. Wikipedia, "Catholic Sex Abuse Cases."
44. Ibid.
45. Ibid.
46. Belluck and Bruni, "Scandals in the Church."
47. Steinhauer, "Film on Pedophile Priest."

here one invokes the question: "What would Jesus say?" Jesus' reply leaves little doubt about what the Church leaders should have done:

> Whoever causes one of these little ones who believe in me to sin, it would be better for him if a great millstone were put around his neck and he were thrown into the sea; what terrible things will come on the world through scandal! It is inevitable that scandal should occur; nonetheless woe to that man through whom scandal comes (Matt 18:6–7).

Such loss of trust by the laity is only part of the damage done to the Church by pedophile priests; the economic strain played a significant part as well. In several archdioceses, bishops were forced into bankruptcy protection as a result of the enormous financial claims and settlements due to victims. For instance, in the archdiocese of Portland, Oregon, bankruptcy suspended civil action in a case involving the trial of a priest who was accused of molesting more than fifty boys.[48] Professor Zech, an expert in Catholic Church finances, told the Associated Press, "For a diocese to give up control of their finances is totally out of character and uncharted."[49] In Boston, where sex abuse scandals resulted in huge claims against the Church, the cardinal sold Church property rather than file bankruptcy and cede control of diocesan finances. Other dioceses that were plagued with the great expense of sexual abuse settlements preferred to deplete their cash savings and reserves rather than file bankruptcy.[50] In 2009 BBC News reported that throughout the US sex abuse cases have cost the Church more than $650 million. Since then, the figure has reached billions of dollars. At the conclusion of all the pending cases, it will cost the Catholic Church of America and Ireland well over the two billion dollar mark in cash settlements.[51] The abuse scandals have more than damaged the moral fiber and authority of the Catholic Church. This crisis has almost broken the economic back of the Church, not just in the United States but in Western Europe as well. These crimes against humanity will continue to haunt Church credibility for years to come. How this crisis may be tempered by openness to dissent and creation of a more open Church is the subject of the next segment of this chapter.

---

48. BBC News, "Sex Claims Bankrupt US Archdiocese."
49. Ibid.
50. Ibid.
51. Ibid.

Inability to Accept Dissent

One evening during class at Manor College, the topic under discussions was centered on dissent and criticism. One student in particular recounted a horrific story worthy of mention. It concerned her thirteen-year-old sister, who was denied the sacrament of confirmation by the pastor of her parish because the child's parents had recently divorced. Needless to say the family was upset, but they had no recourse since the pastor would not alter his decision. In another situation, a young man who aspired to the priesthood applied to Saint Charles Borromeo Seminary but was denied admission because his parents were divorced. What do the actions of the parents have to do with that of their children? While in graduate school, a deacon openly told the class that before he administered Communion to the sick at a hospital he would first ask patients if they were in a state of grace; and if he found they were not, or were divorced without an annulment, he would not administer Communion regardless of patients' state of health. The deacon's story enraged the whole class, including the professor. Stories like this and similar ones are in the thousands. What are people to do when such horror stories affecting Church credibility become a full-blown crisis?

Dissent, criticism, and openness should be the byproducts of good leadership in the Church, if it is to grow as a Church in the Spirit of Jesus Christ. The basic rights of the faithful and a sense of how history and change are intertwined constitute the inner strength of Church teaching. As Karl Rahner has argued:

> For a critical question about the sense of a defined dogma in the faith of the Church is quite different in kind from opposition to the Church's legal, pastoral or liturgical practices; for the Church itself declares that these things are historically conditioned and can be changed.[52]

If the Church is to propagate the gospel in any lasting, meaningful way, it must promote a sufficient level of dissent and criticism by thinking and acting beyond the norm of conformity. Rules can be changed and modified so long as they do not affect the core beliefs of the Church, such as the inner core of the Paschal Mystery centered in the death and resurrection of Jesus the Christ. For the fundamental premise of Church growth does not develop from absolutizing the policies of the past, but by promoting doctrinal developments of the present and future that can be integrated

---

52. Rahner, "Structural Change," in *Theological Investigations* (hereafter *TI*) 20:129.

into the Church's living the gospel of Jesus Christ, which is that of forgiveness, compassion, and understanding toward all. Manmade laws that are designed to enforce conformity, rather than to expand meaning, only serve to hinder freedom of the Spirit. In Jesus' words, every barren branch that does not produce fruit must be pruned (John 15:2).

Presently, the Church seems to be in a personal struggle of attempting to promulgate teachings that have meaning for today's faithful. To achieve this end, it must carefully prune its teaching that inhibits growth and *stifles the Spirit*. As Rahner observed:

> from its own point of view the Church, undoubtedly, desires to become a power which is open to critical questioning; its faith and the basic character which derives from that faith can be grasped only in free assent. And a free assent of this kind is possible only when the actual, specific existence of the assenting person is involved also.[53]

Rahner claimed that the Church is a powerful and political institution that derives its strength from faith and adherence to certain beliefs that will never change. But the credible power that is derived from its beliefs and teachings depends on how those who exercise authority are open to reasonable dissent, criticism, and modification. Those who disagree with rules that have become outdated and with doctrinal assertions that lack credibility have a God-given right to self-expression and freedom to dissent or engage in dialogue aimed at change. Church regulations, to Rahner, are open to question in as much as they are historically conditioned and based on human action. Practices, rituals, and canons that are manmade can be challenged, modified, or expanded to meet the needs of the times.[54] A Catholic Christian has the absolute right to reasonable dissent within the Church if a particular rule, practice, or canon is out of touch with common sense or the well-being of the faithful. But ultra-conservative leadership seldom sees it that way. Their argument is centered in the notion that dissent, criticism, or modification will hinder unity. For ultra-conservative leaders, the Church must speak as one voice and hold fast to beliefs in traditional homogeneous Catholic teachings. It is obvious they are fearful that the Church may suffer severe hardships and possibly split into several factions, though it seems to be happening anyway regardless of the consequences.[55] But does the real

---

53. Ibid., 130.
54. Ibid., 130.
55. Higgins, *Twelve Theological Dilemmas*, 69.

question lie in the loss of control and the weakening of authority for conservatives? Or is it a power they never really had in the first place?

Progressive thinkers, on the other hand, posit reasonable dissent, logical criticism, and realistic modifications despite unrest from conservatives. Those who espouse the notion of more liberal developmental change observe that dissent, criticism, and change may actually bolster the strength and belief of the faithful. They believe that the Church should provoke debate and better understanding by opening its doors to new possibilities that have not existed in the recent past. Dialogue, discussion, and debate for Catholics may actually foster an atmosphere of "charged deliberation rather than a sterile mood of servile acceptance."[56] The *people of God* have a right to speak their mind. If reasonable debate and criticism are suspended by absolute *ecclesiastical fiat*, it may lead the spirit of the laity to drift away even farther than they already have. This situation affecting Church credibility, more than ever, is in crisis as seen by the growth of acculturated Catholics—those who only show up for Mass on holidays, marriages, baptisms, First Communions, Christmas, and Easter.

Conclusion

From the aforementioned, one can reasonably conclude, *a priori*, that the Catholic Church has difficulties to overcome. These are problems that will not easily go away. Improvement usually comes from intelligent planning, reasonable change, and implementation. The Church must get the word of its willingness to adapt to the needs of the faithful. But the heart of the problem lies in the bonds of hierarchical "rigidification,"[57] the loss of control and fear of the unknown. Modernization, growth, and change for the Church will not come by repeating the same old rules and utilizing the same old techniques. Such principles and practices only perpetuate an abundance of the same old results.

I have been an usher at Saint Albert the Great parish in Huntingdon Valley, Pennsylvania, for more than eighteen years at the noon Sunday Mass. During this time, I have seen attendance drop significantly. Whole pews, more often than not, are half empty, when at one time they were mostly close to full. This is a relatively new parish with a wonderful pastor, in a reasonably affluent community with about ten thousand Catholics. At Sunday Mass I

---

56. Ibid., 70.

57. A term borrowed by Edward Schillebeeckx in *Church with a Human Face*, 69.

sometimes look around in astonishment. Where are the people? What can be done to change the slide toward irrelevance and possible oblivion as a Church? Attendance at Sunday Mass in the United States as well in Europe appears to be in a deplorable condition. How is it that Catholics flock to churches on Easter Sunday and Christmas Day but afterwards disappear for the balance of the year, except for perhaps weddings, funerals, and baptisms, etc.? These are difficult questions that demand immediate attention to stem the tide of irrelevance in the life of the faithful the Church now faces. Another calamity that befalls the Church is when bishops close parishes for economic reasons and tell parishioners that there are not enough priests to service the parish. Just today, the six o'clock news reported that Cardinal Justin Regali of Philadelphia announced the closing of Saint Bernard's Parish School in the heart of the Northeast. This parish school is situated in the heart of thousands of homes. Two of my children were baptized there in the parish church. What will happen to the students and their sense of camaraderie and communion within the church community? Closing a parish school seems to be a precipitous step toward closing the parish church.[58]

Unless there is a total change in the community and only a handful of people are left attending Sunday Mass, closing parishes is a no-win situation for the Church. Bishops must consider every aspect of the community in order to keep a parish church open; they must be very sensitive to the pastoral needs of the community and look for every possible way to keep a parish church open before taking action to close its doors forever. Even Abraham had compassion for those living in Sodom when he bargained with God not to destroy the city, even if there were only ten innocent people left (Gen 18:22). Did not God oblige him? Bishops must do the same. The Church is the lifeblood of the *people of God*; it is not just a business where it lives or dies by profit and loss. What the Church gains on one hand it may lose on the other. Although bishops sometimes hide behind the notion that marginally solvent parishes must be closed, perhaps what they are really saying is that there are no priests to run the parish or administer the sacraments. This shortage of priests can be traceable to the lack of vocations. Young men, it seems, are not interested in entering the seminary today. The statistics on this are clear. The core of the problem, no doubt, can be found in the code of celibacy. Why should young men surrender God's gift of marriage to become celibate priests? Is it not possible that married priests can serve the Lord just as well as celibate priests? This is not to say that there

58. Gardner, 6 p.m. TV news report.

are not blessings in the celibate life if a young man is so inclined; but most men who desire to serve the Lord in the priesthood find their attraction to marriage too overpowering to live a celibate life. The truth lies in the statistics: the reality is that one out of every three former Roman Catholic priests in the United States has, in fact, transitioned from celibacy to marriage.[59]

Father Vincent Corso, a married priest, observes that there are twenty thousand men, formerly celibate priests, who are now married and, in most instances, raising families. He goes on to say that for the first twelve centuries of Church history, priests, bishops, and thirty-nine popes were married, and those who were married and those who were celibate worked side by side in service of the faithful.[60] Most of the celibate priests from that era were monks and contemplatives who preferred the life of celibacy and self-sacrifice in the service of Christ.[61] This is a blessing that cannot be denied, but celibacy is not for all men who discover the deep abiding call to serve the Lord in the priesthood. Saint Paul defines this problem clearly: "There are different gifts but the same Spirit; there are different ministries but the same Lord; there are different works but the same God who accomplishes all of them in everyone. To each person the manifestation of the Spirit is given for the common good" (1 Cor 12:4–7). For the ultra-conservative leadership of the Church, the notion of celibacy can become a rigidification of a rule that gets in the way of common sense. It is this which prevents the Church from growing and serving the Lord by opening the door to new possibilities for married men to serve above the level of deacon. It is time to eliminate the inflexibility of the discipline of celibacy in the ministries and to open the door to reasonable dissent and logical criticism aimed at enhancing credibility and attractiveness of the Church in the modern world.

The Church continues to stumble and fall, however, from scandalous pedophile priests. The sexual abuse has threatened even the famed Jesuit universities.[62] The Jesuit province of the Society of Jesus from Oregon has decided to file bankruptcy in the face of hundreds of sexual abuse claims. This moral crisis may jeopardize the financial health of Gonzaga and Seattle Universities as well as other educational institutions that are operated by communities of religious priests like the Jesuits, Franciscans, and other

59. Corso, "Facts about Married Catholic Priests."
60. Ibid.
61. Ibid.
62. Schmalz, "Sex Abuse Claims Threaten Jesuit Universities."

orders.[63] These scandals have caused a weakening of the Church's moral fiber and authoritative standing in the community and the world. When Catholic theologians sit with other denominational confessions in ecumenical dialogue the scandalous acts of so many priests severely hampers their exchanges. How can one sit and talk of unity when one's brothers in the priesthood are abusing the young? This is a disaster for the Catholic Church that no one knows when or how will end.

Without question, the Church needs change and modernization to stem the tide of the crisis it has endured. It is time once again for "agiornamento," and the time to air out and move away from the rigidity of the past. In spite of the work that emanated from Vatican II, more work is needed to continue updating and reforming rituals, practices, and laws of the Church. It could easily slip into the untouchable zone of an ecclesiastical rigor mortis. Without change, the Catholic Church will either disappear in its present form or become, in the future, a mere relic of its past. The message is clear: when Jesus walked the dusty roads of Judea, he was considered a radical, someone advocating change and modernization from an antiquated system of practices that required updating and reform. But now the signs of the times are here, and reform and renewal for the Catholic Church seem immanent. The leadership of the Church must seize this moment in time and return to the message and mission of Jesus Christ, which is that of forgiveness, understanding, love, and compassion to all.

In the following chapter, we will explore possibilities of change and modernization through the prophetic thoughts of Karl Rahner, Geffrey Kelly, and other progressives who love and serve the Lord by loving and serving his Church.

63. Ibid.

2
Shades of Modernity

IN SPITE OF THE Church's hierarchical rigidity and its hesitation to engage in meaningful reform by adapting to the contemporary world, most Roman Catholics still maintain a limited sense of loyalty to the Church. But this endurance of fidelity only goes so far. In fact, scores of the faithful have come to be known as "cultural Catholics," people who have drifted away from the Church and are Catholic in name only. Subsequently, their participation in Church functions is limited to special occasions, for example: Easter Sunday, Christmas Mass, family baptisms, confirmations, First Communions, funerals, and other special Church events, etc. Then suddenly, as with the wave of a magical wand, the huge crowds are no more and the pews of the churches on Sunday are half empty once again. This much is clear: the Church has lost much of its mystique, as evidenced by the recurring crises that has befallen it. From most visible venues, the Catholic Church presently lacks the respect and the appeal it once enjoyed.

Going forward into the future, the Church will either proclaim the good news of Jesus Christ with true humility and dedicated service to others, or run the risk of eventually withering to a level of still unknown proportions. Change, adaptation to the contemporary world, and credible development in the present are essential to recapturing and maintaining the vitality of the Church for the future. This would be a future that will focus on the Word, rather than an absolute rule by the few hierarchs who seem stuck in an idealized past. In any development, the gospel is still foundational to a meaningful growth of the Church that gives sustenance to the life of the faithful. In other words, the Church must never cease to proclaim the gospel and become, as the German pastor and martyr Dietrich Bonhoeffer suggested in his *Letters and Papers from Prison*, a servant Church that "exists for others."[1]

We live in an age of instant information. Statistically, people receive information as quickly as it happens from almost anywhere in the world. News that occurs on one side of the planet is instantly available to all. The world has come from the age of darkness into an unparalleled sphere of light. In sum, the Church exists on the threshold of an innovative modern age. It is now time for the Church to move forward in that direction. The future is rapidly arriving and the time for change and modernization of the Catholic Church is at hand.

Proposals for Change

Theologian Karl Rahner, a guiding force at Vatican Council II and a mentor for the Catholic Church in adapting to the modern world, strongly supports the view that the Church must plan for the future if it expects to thrive and grow. It is a well-known axiom that "failing to plan is planning to fail." Effectively, like any other large institution, the Church must plan ahead. In Rahner's words:

> The gospel warning against taking too much thought for the morrow therefore holds also at the present time. But for what can be foreseen we should still prepare at the opportune time and not simply go on as before and wait like a mouse, hypnotized by the serpent of the future and doing nothing to save itself.[2]

As a proactive theologian, Rahner urges the Church to cover its place in the modern world by planning and anticipating events that could possibly alter its well-being and ultimate mission in the imminent future. Rahner takes the position that it is proper for the Church to look into the foreseeable future and attempt to prevent potential problems that could undermine its ultimate mission. He criticizes those who would hide behind the barriers of ultra-conservatism, arguing that it is important to ward off potential trouble in the future through the implementation of intelligent

---

1. Bonhoeffer, *Letters and Papers from Prison*, 381.
2. Rahner, *Shape of the Church to Come*, 48.

planning and modification in the present. To Rahner, for a church to act like a "timid mouse that is stymied at the thought of change" and modernization is to take a step backward in time and to enter into the darkness of stagnation.[3] Indeed, it takes courage to abandon present-day positions that represent out-of-date thinking that is no longer tenable for those seeking the highest good of the Church,[4] namely, that of saving souls from "*the hell of meaninglessness, of obsession, . . . of self-destructive futilities*" that befalls present-day civilization.[5] If those in the Church who stand at the forefront of leadership ignore "*the signs of the time*," the structure of the Church could crumble at its very foundations.[6] The Church exists in the age of technology that is full of statistical and scientific information, and as such, the leaders of the Church, if they so desire, could seriously examine the trends, the opportunities, and the potential problems that may occur in the Church for many years into the foreseeable future. Rahner offers Church leaders this invaluable suggestion: "Plans for the future must be made at the opportune time."[7] For example, the leaders of the Church already know that within ten years or so the Church may face an enormous shortage of priests to operate the parishes. Common sense would dictate that the problem must be addressed immediately, much the same as taking preventive medicine prior to the onset of illness.

Statistically, it is well known that the number of priests has been dwindling at crisis proportions. Who is going to manage the existing parishes, let alone those of the future? The Church leaders must, in fact, take preventative action in the now to avert a future dilemma. Rahner insists that "this is intelligent planning in order to meet the state of affairs which will soon be with us."[8] He goes on to say that men who are married and worthy of ordination to the priesthood can make up for the lack of celibate priests. He is convinced, as many others, that a time is coming when this change will be absolutely necessary in order for parishes to exists in the future life of the Church. But he sternly warns those who would oppose such a notion that if we wait another ten or twenty years before making a decision to alleviate the deficiency of priests, there may be havoc in the Church of

3. Ibid., 46.
4. Ibid., 49.
5. Thomas Merton, *Love and Living*, 4 (emphasis added).
6. Rahner, *Shape of the Church to Come*, 49 (emphasis added).
7. Ibid., 50.
8. Ibid., 50.

the future, for no one will be ready, willing, or able to carry out the duties and responsibilities of parish life.[9] To Rahner, the present is the time for the leadership to act.

Theologian Geffrey Kelly, a strong proponent for change and modernization in the Church, has observed that people who experience dissatisfaction within the Catholic Church share a common hope for the rebirth of Catholicity. This would be the dawn of a new Church that will not tolerate the notion of ceremonial pontification, but rather, move to create a more humble Church that will take up the cause of "servant leadership" in the faith, hope, and charity of Jesus Christ.[10] Kelly goes on to say that if the Church is to retain its true link with its origins and attempt to emulate the compassionate and redemptive service of Jesus Christ, it must become what it started out to be, namely, a servant Church for all to embrace. In other words, the Church should become gospel-centered, as opposed to the ceremonial and ritualistic institution it presently lends itself to be. The Church should return to the practices of its origins, which is the proclamation of the mission and message of Jesus Christ in true service and humility. And above all, it must place its immense resources at the service of the poor, the anguished, and the abused, by becoming heralds of the gospel ideals, especially as they relate to Jesus' known deference for the suffering and the outcast.[11]

Rahner contends that the Church should be "declericalized,"[12] a term that for him goes to the heart of its leadership, explicitly, the office-holders who pontificate and sometimes lord their authority over the meek. He recognizes the value of the hierarchy in the Church, its powers, its duties, and functions, but he takes it to a higher level and holds that their powers, duties, and functions must be defined according to their ongoing responsibilities and obligations, tasks that should be categorically distinguished and shared among both clergy and laity. To Rahner, the functions and powers bestowed upon the office-holders in the concrete can or must be precisely conceived and set out in a power-sharing manner.[13] Rahner suggests that there are two differing types of hierarchical leadership in the Church, and claims that

> Office holders in the Church have a functional character in the Church as society, even though its functions constitutes a sign of

9. Ibid., 51.
10. Kelly, "Futurists and Reformers," 70.
11. Kelly quotes McBrien, *Do We Need the Church?*, 75.
12. Rahner, *Shape of the Church to Come*, 56.
13. Ibid., 56.

what is real in the Church: the free Spirit, faith, hope, and love, to which all socially institutional factors in office are orientated, and at the same time are never identical with them. Hence the 'hierarchy' in the real nature of the Church is not identical with the hierarchy in the Church's social structure.[14]

What Rahner means is that, presently in the hierarchal Church, there are two types of office-holders. There are those, in the nature of the Church, who practice the notion of servant leadership and live in faith, hope, and charity for the sake of the gospel; they are the leaders who are not self-serving and who are filled with humility, love their sisters and brothers, and have and maintain a prophetic message for all. These office-holders, according to Rahner, constitute the real Church. They are unselfish and far from being identified solely with their official position and official titles.[15] On the other hand, there are office-holders who function in the Church's social structure and who seem full of themselves as they emulate the posture of self-importance. They appear to be filled with sanctimonious pride and act with superiority by virtue of their office. They sometimes lord their princely title over the faithful and the humble. In this connection, Tom Stella, a priest in the Congregation of the Holy Cross, tells an interesting story about a bishop who was visiting a friend's mother in a nursing facility. While the bishop was sitting in the parlor next to an older woman, during a break, he turned and asked the old woman, "Do you know who I am?" The elderly lady studied him intently for a moment, and then said, "No! But if you go to the front desk they can tell you there."[16] Stella goes on to say that when we make the mistake of identifying ourselves with our functions, we soon feel inhibited and limited by them. We become what we think we are, not who we really are. In the case of this bishop, obviously he was puffed up by his own princely ego that made him look rather small, instead of a humble servant of the Christ.[17] Rahner equates the dichotomy of office-holders with a simple metaphor and makes the following analysis:

> The situation in the Church is really like that of a chess club. Those who really support the club and give it its meaning are the members, to the extent that they play chess well. The hierarchy of the club leadership is necessary and appropriate if and as far as it

14. Ibid., 56.
15. Ibid., 56–57.
16. Stella, *The God Instinct*, 28.
17. Ibid., 28–29.

serves the community of chess players and their 'hierarchy,' and does not think it is identical with the latter or that it can play chess better simply by virtue of its function.[18]

With the different attitudes that are displayed in these two types of office-holders, Rahner believes that "it will take a miracle from the Spirit of God to prevent an absolute schism."[19] To Rahner, as soon as the obvious dogmatic truths are lived and practiced impartially and taken for granted by office-holders and Christians, we will have a "declericalized Church."[20] This would be a Church where priests can retain their importance but minister in equality with others, a Church where celibacy is no more and priests are free to marry if they so desire, a Church that is open to the priesthood for women, a Church where those who hold office practice the message of the gospel with true humility and service to others. Only when the hierarchy crosses this threshold and walks into the light will the Church become declericalized for the sake of the gospel and the benefit and growth of Catholic Christianity.[21]

Rahner makes the even bolder statement that "The task for the Church is to exist for others, and not for itself."[22] This statement parallels Jesus' teaching, "The Sabbath was made for man, not man for the Sabbath" (Mark 2:27). When the Church exists for others, it finds itself in communion with the mission and message of none other than Jesus Christ and called to a ministry of loving and serving all. For it is only in serving others—that is, the poor, the aged, the sick, the abused, and the voiceless—that the Church will be a Church for others, and thus continue in the goodness of God's compassionate will.

From another perspective, theologian-martyr Dietrich Bonhoeffer observes that religion should never be equated with "faith" as God's gift; for religion with its institutional structures, petty regulations, and layers of laws is all too human. For Bonhoeffer, religious structures are sometimes filled with fear and are prone to sin.[23] Religion's trappings of faith are never the same as the gift of faith whereby God saves his sinful children and

---

18. Rahner, *Shape of the Church to Come*, 56.
19. Ibid., 57.
20. Ibid., 57.
21. Ibid., 57.
22. Ibid., 61.
23. Kelly and Nelson, *Cost of Moral Leadership*, 42.

bestows the genuine holiness that flows from faith.[24] Only religion that reflects the deepest relationship with Jesus Christ is the religion that inspires compassion, love, and service toward all.[25] What Bonhoeffer is saying is that organized religion can be flawed and prone to sin by human behavior, including pride, ambition, and the authoritarian aspects we often see in the Catholic Church. It is no secret that the Church *has always been a church of sinners*; for all are sinners who, at times, can be bent on petty jealousies, political machinations, and other human weaknesses that make persons less than human. But Bonhoeffer suggests that the Church has a mandate to preserve the mysteries of the Christian faith that were proclaimed by Jesus Christ—not with a pathetic, defensive frenzy, or ceremonial pomposity, but rather with prayer, worship, and a Christ-like example for all to see and emulate.[26] In other words, the Church fathers must set the example to be Christ-like, for they represent the living God, and their minds and hearts are to mirror the image of Christ the Lord.[27]

Yet from another viewpoint, German scholar Johann Baptist Metz claims that the hierarchy of Church often appears slanted on catering to the rich and powerful bourgeois to the exclusion of the messianic mission to the poor. In his study *The Emergent Church*, Metz observes that, "In the Christianity of our time, the messianic religion of the Bible has largely been changed into a bourgeois religion."[28] This is an observation, he believes, that is not intended to embarrass or unduly criticize the bourgeois, or the petty bourgeois who have made Church life what it is in Europe,[29] but rather the very idea of a bourgeois religion, which can be a real threat to Christianity in the future. For the Church's actions and lifestyle apparently fail to recognize and affirm the difference between the messianic religion of Jesus Christ and the material religion of the present day hierarchs who govern it.[30] To Metz, as a result of the bourgeois attitudes of the Roman Curia, the messianic Church of the future may be in grave danger. He claims that this is not from the view that it may be guilty of merely pacifying or consoling the poor, or becoming what Karl Marx has called religion the "opium for the masses,"

24. Ibid., 42.
25. Ibid., 41.
26. Ibid., 43.
27. Ibid., 43.
28. Metz, *Emergent Church*, 1–2.
29. Ibid., 1.
30. Ibid., 2.

but rather, from the Church's imminent danger of catering to the rich and powerful aristocrats—those whom the Church hopes to accommodate.[31]

Metz goes on to say that if the Church of the future follows the bourgeois route, it will likely cause a substantial disruption in its Catholicity. He claims, therefore, that "The meaning of love cuts across the meaning of having."[32] In a sense, the Church must mend its ways by adhering to the messianic message of unselfish love if it is to survive and flourish in the future. For the poor, the abused, and those who live in utter poverty *will inherit the kingdom of God* that Jesus had proclaimed. Metz observes that Jesus' teaching with respect to love is far more important that the wealth and riches of the bourgeois. Jesus' new commandment is clear: "we should love one another" (John 13:34–35) and not just cater only to the rich and powerful who control the purse strings of the world, but serve everyone, even those who have nothing of value to offer the Church.[33]

Metz seems to believe that the transformation of society is not the primary concern of the gospel and certainly not the mission of the Church. Rather, to him, the task of the Church is to seek out and save the lost souls of Christ, by changing its dated policies and adapting the conversion of hearts.[34] For the messianic message of Christ is the primary cause for the proclamation of Christianity and reaches farther than the eyes can behold. This to Metz is the most radical and challenging form of reform. Changing hearts to become more Christ-like, by living the message of the Holy One of God, is the true and only conversion. Thus, by reaching deeply into the spirit of those that are deprived and disappointed with the Church, the leadership can redefine itself by the love it shares with others through its ministry of conversion in the manner of the gospel teaching of Jesus Christ.[35] But Metz has misgivings over the present attitude of the Church leadership, which may, he fears, spill into the future. His intuition tells him that the Church hesitates to move in this direction of Christ's piety and *agapeic* love, with the resultant change of hearts that would restart Church credibility in the modern world. He realizes to his chagrin that human nature, slanted toward the rigidity of attitudes, is incredibly difficult to adapt to a rapidly changing technological world, a world that is reinforced by less

31. Ibid., 2.
32. Ibid., 2.
33. Ibid., 2.
34. Ibid., 2.
35. Ibid., 2.

than Christ-like ecclesial leadership.³⁶ The crisis of life, as he sees it, is that much of the hierarchy will not have a change of heart, but the absence of this change has been further concealed under the appearance of structural changes of a superficially believed-in but not genuinely lived-in faith.³⁷ For Metz, "merely *believed-in faith*"³⁸ is superficial and far different from a faith that is *deep and abiding*, which is the faith that converts the soul. He considers the difference between living their lives as disciples or just believing in discipleship, for the two can be contradictory to one another. True disciples live and practice the gospel in the service to others, whereas those who merely believe in discipleship often limit their faith to the abstract notion of ecclesiocentric beliefs in Church doctrines; for it is one thing to be a disciple, and quite another to merely believe in the concept of discipleship. Conversely, this is the difference between calling oneself a Christian and alternatively being *Christ-like*.³⁹ Metz goes on to challenge the Church and argues, "Do we show real love to others, or do we just believe in love? For under the cloak of belief in love remains the same egotistical conformists we have always been?"⁴⁰ Obviously, his questions are Christocentric and he makes a case against those in the Church who are indifferent to the message and mission of Christ embodied in his new commandment to "love one another" (John 13:34)—and not cater just to the rich. This word of Christ underscores the attitude of a leadership who conforms to the notion of a bourgeois religion while at the same time lording it over the poor and abused while unconsciously ignoring those that suffer unjustly.⁴¹ Metz is convinced that there must be reconciliation between the conservatives and the liberals of the Catholic Church. Those who control the Church, whether conservative or liberal, must prioritize the task of ending the disparity between the poor and the rich in the Church as a whole. And by doing so they make a Christ-like effort to end our troubled world where mainstream churches give only the appearances of unity, but take no concrete steps toward effectuating that unity among the followers for whom Jesus prayed before his death "that they may be one as we are one" (John 17:23).⁴²

36. Ibid., 2.
37. Ibid., 3.
38. Ibid., 3.
39. Ibid., 3.
40. Ibid., 3.
41. Ibid., 3.
42. Ibid., 11.

Glimpse of the Future

In a study of futurists and their vision to help institutions save themselves from the hell of meaninglessness, theologian Geffery Kelly notes that the need for people with a view toward the future to facilitate change in the Church and to help it save itself from the anguish of conformity and stagnation. In this vision, certain theologians are able to enunciate how the Church should learn to exist in the awareness of new possibilities for growth, change, and modernization that can make any future hopeful.[43] The task for Church futurists is not to modify the gospel, but to formulate assessments and take advantage of opportunities in the not too distant future for the benefit and growth of Catholic Christianity. No doubt, to interpret potential events in the future always comes with it a certain amount of risk. And yet, in light of the consequences, intelligent planning for what may lie ahead is principal to the sustenance in the life of the Church.[44] Kelly, like Rahner, believes that intelligent planning is necessary in order for the Church to look beyond the next ten to twenty years or more. Preparation for the future is essential for the Church to survive in a world that is becoming more and more businesslike and secularized by the day.

People live today in a world of violence, greed, and sensuality. All one has to do is to turn on the evening news to witness the pseudo-values of secularism that are corrupting the morals of the nation's youth. In order for the Church to grow into the future, it must change and modernize by returning to the basic principles of a gospel-centered Church where love, forgiveness, and service to the poor are its essential primordial goals. Kelly concludes, "It is tempting to think that the future of the Church, because of critical judgment, may be optimistic; and that it may finally become a structure of hope within the national, and local communities."[45] He goes on to say that for the Church to become an inspiration it is mandatory to change and modernize its antiquated thinking, by reexamining rituals and renewing many of the practices that are capable of disillusioning both the clergy in the parishes and the faithful. Essentially, the Church must move in the direction of a new *reformation*, a change that makes it easier for the

---

43. Kelly and Nelson, *Cost of Moral Leadership*, 70.
44. Ibid., 71. Kelly quotes Kenski, *Religious Factor*.
45. Ibid., 71.

faithful to recognize the divine love and fellowship, which should inspire ecclesial restructuring and communion with all Christians.[46]

In this context, Kelly is convinced that "An uncertain future beckons the Church to become, as it always should have been, an *ecclesia simper reformanda*,"[47] an ecclesial Church that is always reforming and reinventing itself, as the Book of Revelation declares: "'See I make all things new,' says the Lord" (Rev 21:5–6). Kelly goes on to say that "it would be a tragedy if the leadership of the Church should be dragged-down kicking and screaming into the modern world."[48] Indeed, the Church will suffer dire consequences in the future if it does not change and modernize in the present by returning to the gospel-centered community of Jesus Christ. The Church must, in effect, prepare for the promised future in the present.

Karl Rahner likewise observes that if we speak of the Church's future, the obvious question arises as to which church we are talking about: the Western church, the Latin American church, the church of Africa, or the world Church?[49] To him the answer is clear: he proposes the view that "all Christian Churches are the same . . . and yet, they are different."[50] He goes on to say that although there may be striking differences in the churches of the future, there may be, for example, problems envisioning the outcome for the church of Europe. Presently, that church is dwindling, for it seems to be losing its center of influence. To Rahner, the longevity of the European church can only be predicted with difficulty, or not at all. He supports the notion that if the torch of faith, hope, and love should fall in Europe, then the Church in other parts of the world will pick up the cause and carry the Christian banner. For God alone is the future of all Christianity and none other.[51] It seems to Rahner, therefore, that unless the Catholic churches of the world are forced into uniformity as the one Holy Catholic Apostolic Church, there will always be healthy differences, depending on the continent, where the Church is situated, and how the Church in that part of the world practices its faith. In other words, the individual churches of the world, although united by the Spirit of Christ, will develop their own unique methods, canons, and practices of honoring and praising God, ac-

---

46. Ibid., 71.
47. Ibid., 71.
48. Ibid., 71. Kelly quotes Dulles, *Models of the Church*.
49. Rahner, "Future of the Church," *TI* 20:113.
50. Ibid., 113.
51. Ibid., 113–14.

cording to their own cultural and environmental norms, irrespective of the standing of the European Church and other more far-flung churches. According to Rahner, as long as Christianity has not achieved complete unity, it seems inevitable that there will be cultural shades and contrasts in the various local churches throughout the world.[52] One church's opportunities, challenges, and practices will not necessarily be the same as those of another. But for Rahner, this is not the most serious question of all. What is important to him is the viability of Christianity in a secularized world of the present.[53]

It appears that Rahner's main concern, with respect to Christianity in the future, is the growth of pluralism, where Christians are moving away from outdated thinking, practices, and authority, modeled after the Western European church. This church, it seems, is no longer in the mainstream of Christian life as it had been in the past. Moreover, people are shifting toward a more secular way of life and their thoughts and actions are far removed from the Church's authoritarian control. Possibly this change is the result of its failure to keep up with the times, or perhaps this transformation is caused by the modernization and more advanced education of the world's population. Whatever the reason, there seems to be cause for genuine concern.[54]

If Rahner is correct in his assessment, then the only way to avert problems in the Church of the future is to center on the notion of effective planning and reasonable implementation by the leaderships of the Church in the present. The Church must plan for tomorrow, today, by returning to the roots of Christianity with determination. Rahner calls for all Christians to be united together for one purpose and that is the dissemination among all peoples of the gospel of Jesus Christ. This is so because we live in a rational and technologically advanced civilization where the individual parts are increasingly growing and decaying into a unity and common destiny. This is a development that is marked by militant atheism that could become an imminent threat to all peoples. To Rahner, then, if we refer to the future of the Catholic Church, in the last resort, we are actually looking to the development of an ecumenical spirit of Christianity, its unity, and wholeness in the future.[55] The future of such a worldwide Catholic Church can only be

52. Ibid., 104.
53. Ibid., 104.
54. Ibid., 104.
55. Ibid., 104.

assimilated by understanding its nature, faith, and theological correctness. For the Church's ultimate nature is absorbed by the social, historical, and structured community of those who believe in Christ crucified and raised from the dead as the definitive and victorious self-promise of the one and living God to the world. Hence, to Rahner: "the Church is the basic sacrament of salvation to the world."[56] It promises God's salvation, which can only be comprehended by faith in God's mysterious grace, even in parts of the world where the Church itself has not yet been established.

Rahner's Concept of the Future

If we are to study the possibilities of the future Catholic Church, Rahner posits, "We must not say simply that it has a future,"[57] for we know very little or nothing about the nature and possibilities of the future Church. He goes on to say that even the predictions of sociologists, philosophers, and futurologists are highly problematic in their analysis of the Church's future. Although it is presently possible to determine the growth and decline of populations with a degree of statistical certitude, Rahner's observation is that we cannot predict with any amount of conviction how and what the Church will look like in the next few decades. This *unforeseeability* of the future Church is particularly relevant in light of the growth and decline of the secular world. In the first place, we know little or nothing from the historical movement of the secular world. Yet this information is vital for the growth of the Church. Secondly, the Church is centered on the notion of faith and salvation, which is governed by God's gift of freedom, and the free will that may affect people's well-being.[58] Even though we cannot predict the Church's concrete future, Rahner says it is possible to predict that "the Church's future will be different in many respects from the present."[59] For "change and endurance"[60] is the paramount nature of the Church. He goes on to say that it is obvious we cannot humanly analyze the changeable from the permanent in the future historical context of the Church; nor is it possible to know in advance where the dividing line is situated between the perishing and the unwavering. But what we do know is that however

---

56. Ibid., 104.
57. Ibid., 108.
58. Ibid., 108.
59. Ibid., 109.
60. Ibid., 109.

much the Church may change in the future, it will always remain the same through the Spirit of Christ. Nevertheless, according to Rahner, "We can safely say that the Church of the future will look very different from that of today."[61] He claims further that the center of the world Church is no longer in Europe. The core of Christianity that once was is now far removed from the Western praxis of the Church's officialdom. He views the world Church, since it presently appears to exist, as a body detached from the realm of European control, which cannot and will not emulate the *"lifestyle, law, liturgy, and theology"* of Roman influence.[62] Churches from other parts of the world presently maintain the notion of cultural independence that is distanced from European ways of practicing Christianity as a God-given right to autonomy. However, since the Catholic churches of the world are separated from the European ways and maintain a lifestyle of their own, they are still somewhat connected to the Church's present structures, including the papacy. Hence, to Rahner: In this world-Church, according to our Catholic faith, there will always be a Petrine ministry with its permanent and perhaps in some respects increasingly important tasks. Nevertheless, in the concrete way in which this ministry is exercised, a great deal will be changed, can be changed, and must be changed.[63]

He observes that popes for many centuries exercised the Petrine ministry over the world Church. But this ministry was generally limited to that of the Western church alone. When the Church began to grow and flourish in other parts of the world, these new ministries expressed the deep desire for independence from Roman authority. They preferred to worship God through Jesus Christ in their individual cultural way without the need for Roman intervention or control. To these churches, the pope's function as the patriarch of the West has and will remain a venerable position, and will have a less important role in the world Church as a whole.[64]

To Rahner, the Second Vatican Council marked the beginning of a new and historical dialogue for the Catholic Church with all Christianity. Rahner notes that this is only "the beginning of this dialogue and not its end."[65] He sees this new position of the Council not as a *faint-hearted* compromise with any sort of spirit of the age, but rather, an ongoing process

---

61. Ibid., 109.
62. Ibid., 110.
63. Ibid., 111.
64. Ibid., 111.
65. Ibid., 111.

that embraces the view that it must take the form of a critical and absolute opposition to a godless and greedy consumer mentality that is largely drained of authentic human emotion.[66] It is true that this process of change and rejuvenation for the Church must include more than mere superficial dialogue. It must include the transformation of its lifestyle and become more considerate of the treatment of the laity who has finally come of age. The Church must also search for new and better ways of proclaiming the written word of the Gospels, for it must always recognize and respect God's gift of "freedom of conscience," even while declaring the apparent workings and proclamations of the Church's officialdom.[67] But Rahner assures us that, in this unavoidably changing Church, there exists the permanence of Christianity—that which will never change: the death and resurrection of Jesus Christ and the inspiration of the gospel teachings of Jesus that will outlive every form of change and modernization even unto the end of time. The gospel word of Christ continues to be as fresh and new as it was lived and taught some two thousand years ago.

> This message is not subject to time and time's changes, since it is itself the proclamation of the end of all time, since in the last resort and properly speaking it does not say that something remains of what we have now, that we are not deprived of our possessions: what it does say is that the absolute future—-which is the eternal God himself, beyond all limits of time—-will reach us as the fulfillment of time and history, whether the course of the changing times is long or short, whether it is filled with victories or with defeats.[68]

Thus, for Rahner, the essence and foundation of Christianity, namely, the death and resurrection of Jesus Christ, will never change or modernize, but will stand the test of time, even to the end of the world, for it contains "the pure infinity of God as the absolute future of humanity."[69]

It is obvious then, the future of the Church is filled with uncertainty. Planning could be speculative just as a journey into the future is a voyage into the unknown. What is certain to Rahner, however, as it is to all believing Christians, is that the Word of the Lord will proceed on its course even to the end of time, and not even the gates of hell will prevail over those who

---

66. Ibid., 111.
67. Ibid., 111.
68. Ibid., 112.
69. Ibid., 112–13.

believe that Jesus Christ is Lord and Savior (Matt 16:18).[70] This for Rahner and all Christianity is the "*confident assurance*" of things to come. For the eschatological goal of the Catholic Christian is not the Church itself, but rather the "kingdom of God."[71]

Return of the Faithful

The notion of bringing back the faithful to a more authentic Church community is an inviting concept that, no doubt, is on the lips and thoughts of the Church hierarchy. But how can this goal become accomplished? What is necessary once again to fill the churches with people of faith? Performing the same old tactics in the same old way will, no doubt, accomplish the same old results. But the more pressing question is this: what will the hierarchy do to bring back the faithful who are standing on the sidelines of Catholicism?

Karl Rahner has developed a profound and practical concept that may be used as a first step in returning "sideline" Catholics back into the fold of practicing the faith. His observation is highlighted by the view "we must be a Church with open-doors."[72] Opening the doors to the Church can be the first essential step in the process of bringing back those who have migrated from Catholicism. For various reasons, these are often the disgruntled Catholics who are rarely seen at Sunday Mass. He goes on to say that in former times, when life was described in "social and religio-sociological terms,"[73] the Church could be divided into several distinct classes: those who were baptized and those who were not. Many of those who were baptized have been good practicing Catholics, and for the most part have remained true to the faith. On the other hand, those who were baptized Catholic and have drifted away because they were either disillusioned or disappointed with the Church may have decided to profess their faith in Christ by joining another Christian denomination. These people may have concluded that Catholicism was just not for them anymore. Then there are still others who are known as the baptized but "periodic or cultural" Catholics, who show up for Mass at Christmas and Easter Sunday, or possibly a wedding or other ceremonial event. And then, finally, there are the Catholics who were excommunicated by ecclesiastical fiat and are hesitant or embarrassed to

70. Rahner, "Perspectives for the Future of the Church," *TI* 12:202.
71. Ibid., 202 (emphasis added).
72. Rahner, *Shape of the Church to Come*, 71.
73. Ibid., 71.

return to the fold. Whatever the cause for those who have left the Church, it is not important at this juncture. What is paramount at this point is this: how can the hierarchy of the Church bring most if not all of those lost Christians back home? For Rahner the answer is clear: "the Church should treat these various groups as though they were equal."[74] In other words, all could be welcomed back to the Roman Catholic Church, following Jesus' attitude toward sinners and his teaching on forgiveness. To Rahner and the many, the Church must take into account the fluidity and indefiniteness of its frontiers, and realize that, from the top of the hierarchy to the least of the laity, the Church is a body of sinners, and as such, a means to the kingdom of God for all the faithful saints and sinners alike. So it is therefore critical for the Church to *open its doors* in order to survive and become once again more welcoming to the banquet table of Christ, by calling the sheep that have drifted away. Moreover, it is expedient for the leaders of Catholicism to practice forgiveness, love, understanding, and compassion, and to welcome into their spiritual home all with open hearts and open doors. The Church must invite those who have drifted away, for whatever reason, and bring them home as though they had never left. This includes even those who can no longer be identified with the Church through their faith, but still regard the Roman Catholic Church with a sense of positive goodwill as the concrete bearer of the Christian way.[75] In this regard, Rahner declares:

> If love of neighbor requires us to treat no one as an enemy in the ultimate meaning of the word, then Christians are certainly permitted and morally required to consider these marginal settlers as brothers, without suggesting at every turn that they are not really in the Church and not Christians in the true sense.[76]

Rahner claims that all Christians presently in or out of favor with the Church are still sisters and brothers in Christ. We are all united as one in the Spirit through the Christ-centered bond of love, whether people are aware of it or not. For love demands that we treat no one in an adversarial way, or to assume an attitude of self-righteousness. Rather, our sisters and brothers must be respected and cared for with the Christ-like approach of humility and understanding to those who have "fallen away." Rahner's belief in opening the doors of the Church may be a good start in returning many of those who have turned away from Catholicism.

74. Ibid., 73.
75. Ibid., 73.
76. Ibid., 74.

Shades of Modernity

A Church with "opens doors" must readily open itself by eliminating any likeness of a "ghetto-like mentality";[77] meaning that the Church's hierarchical tunnel-vision thinking is frequently tightly wrapped in an impermeable and immutable fortress within a *little box of conformity*. Edward Schillebeeckx refers to this attitude as "rigidification,"[78] the inability to be flexible from one's old ways of thinking.

For Rahner, such ghetto-like thinking is a reflection of the sterile pseudo-orthodoxy, or rather a "purification" of hierarchical laws by administrative means.[79] In other words, the hierarchy legitimizes the Church's pharisaic rules and binding regulations by administrative measures, and then calls them law, without deviation or consideration for those they most affect. These legalistic tactics seem to be a means to control and exclude, rather than function as a means to perpetuate the Word of the gospel. This to Rahner would not sustain the notion of a Church akin to the Lord's followers in accord with the Acts of the Apostles as the "little flock" of Jesus. Instead, such an exclusive Church would seem more like a sect with a ghetto-like mentality. Anyone who does not belong to this faction is considered an enemy to be chastised.[80] Therefore, to Rahner, "If the Church is not to become, to some extent, a sect of this kind, it must become and remain an open-Church."[81] An open Church to Rahner is a Church that is receptive and responsive to all questions with respect to orthodoxy and beliefs it still holds as sound doctrine. The Catholic Church leadership must be open to reasonable change when there is overwhelming support from theologians, clerics, and laity who are capable of critically reviewing the laws, rules, and practices of the Church that seem unreasonable for the time or unfaithful to the teachings and example of Jesus Christ. One prime example is the concrete view of the Church's canon on celibacy and the rules against married priests. These laws seem to be archaic and in need of revision to meet the needs and mission of the Church going forward into the future.[82] Such reforms might also apply to divorced Catholics who remarry after a

---

77. Ibid., 75.
78. Schillebeeckx, *Church with a Human Face*, 69.
79. Rahner, *Shape of the Church to Come*, 93.
80. Ibid., 93.
81. Ibid., 94.
Ibid., 93.
Ibid., 93.
82. Ibid., 95.

failed sacramental marriage, as long as they stand by their second marriage. An open Church, with true forgiveness, would administer the sacraments to them as well.[83]

Rahner's open Church concept also would never support the solidification of paralyzing guilt in the life of Christians. Hanging the threat of mortal sin, damnation, or even excommunication is not the best way to win back souls into the Church. No doubt there are thousands of good Christians who bear the burden of guilt for missing Mass, not fulfilling their so-called "Easter duty," or not adhering to the Church's standard rules of behavior in the sacrament of penance neurosis.[84] Guilt can never be part of an open Church. Nor does an open Church publicly criticize politicians on matters of conscience, by forbidding them the Eucharist and announcing it publicly via the media. An open Church does not condemn the president of the world's strongest country for his position on controversial issues such as stem-cell research or abortion without reproving those same officeholders, past and present, for illegal aggression, unjustified war, violence in the streets, injustice in the workplace, or hunger and starvation in the poorer nations of the world. An open Church is consistent in its moral outlook and assumes the Christ-like attitude of love, forgiveness, understanding, and compassion to all. This is the Rahnerian notion of an open Church, a practical way to bring back the faithful who have strayed from Roman Catholicism for reasons mentioned above.

Is There a Place for Women in the Priesthood?

Robert Kennedy once said, "There are those who look at things the way they are, and ask why. . . . I dream of things that never were and ask, why not?" If that were so, then why are women barred by the Roman Catholic Church from serving in the ministry of the priesthood? Women who are convinced they have a priestly calling are perfectly capable and quite often better suited than men in the service of the priesthood. The answer to this recurring question often runs deeper than the depths of humanity's soul and wider than the galaxies of the universe. In other words, there appears to be no logically significant reason for women not to be ordained to the priesthood, other than uncertainties in the leadership of the Church, including fear of the unknown, loss of control, discrimination, sexism, and

83. Ibid., 95.
84. Ibid., 95.

all that could possibly threaten the patriarchal/hierarchical structure of the Catholic Church centered in the Vatican.[85]

According to Edward Schillebeeckx, "Christian feminism painfully feels the dualism between the liberating hope given by the gospel on the one hand and the enslaving patriarchal structures of the hierarchical Church on the other."[86] How is it, then, that in this new age of human equality the Church insists that only those of the male gender be ordained to *holy orders* of the priesthood? It seems to make little sense, especially in light of the fact that the number of priests in the Church is dwindling at an alarming rate. This is a crisis of immense proportions for the future well-being of the Church. Schillebeeckx goes on to say that, particularly in North America, women's discontent within the Roman Catholic Church is so acute and intense that they have organized a women's movement that intentionally accuses the patriarchal masculine hierarchy in the Church of sexual discrimination.[87]

With respect to the issue of women priests, Karl Rahner has observes that the Church's thinking on this matter may have outlived its usefulness. All one has to do is look at the Church's history in order to determine its stoic thinking. For example, Rahner points to the history of the Church's religious attitudes that were set into law. He reminds the leadership of its past and points out the following elements of its own history: "Recall the institution of slavery during the first Christian centuries, polygamy and the laws of war in the Old Testament, or the Church's prohibition of usury until well into the eighteenth century."[88] Laws, he concludes, that are now obsolete and non-existent but were once considered absolute and unchangeable can be modified over the course of history. There seems to be no logical reason that could prevent the Church from moving in the direction of ordaining women into the priesthood. He notes the documented fact that "there is continual change in the course of history"[89]; the transformation of the Church is no exception, for change is part of the human experience in the flow of life.

The focus of Rahner's theory on the subject of women in the priesthood is centered on the October 15, 1976, *Declaration on the Question of*

---

85. Meehan, Doko, and Rue, *Brief Overview of Women* Priests, 1.
86. Schillebeeckx, "Discontent among Women," *Church with the Human Face*, 236.
87. Ibid., 226–27.
88. Rahner, "Women and the Priesthood," *TI* 20:42.
89. Ibid., 42.

the *Admission of Women to the Ministerial Priesthood*. This document was sanctioned by the Sacred Congregation for the Doctrine of Faith (CDF) and sealed with the approval of Pope Paul VI. Its content was supposed to end all proposals for women from entering the priestly ministry. Despite the papal seal of approval, Rahner claims that the Declaration is not a closed case and the matter of the ordination of women to the priesthood can be revisited sometime in the future. He argues against this Declaration and claims that "it is in principle reformable, and it can be erroneous."[90] The Declaration contains six points that outline the reasons for excluding women from the priesthood, and Rahner has refuted them all simply because each reason is flawed and misguided. For him, theologians have the right and duty to examine all the arguments contained in any decree from the hierarchy. They must assume that if their examination produces a negative result, as in this case, the basic thesis of the Declaration can itself be questioned and even impugned as flawed.[91] From the outset, in analyzing the Declaration, Rahner claims that a number of questions were excluded that should have been raised in connection with the hierarchical findings; these include questions that emerge from a secular anthropology of the sexes, questions from the history of civilization, and questions from an analysis of modern society with its demand for equality of the sexes, and so forth and so on.[92]

In the first of the six reasons for excluding women from the priestly service, the Declaration refers to "The Church's Constant Tradition," which, according to Church history, has indisputably and uniformly excluded women from the priestly ministry. To Rahner, this point clearly repeats the belief that the tradition of an all-male priesthood transmits a "divine" revelation in the strictest sense. He goes on to say that since there is obviously a purely human tradition in the Church, as in the case of the male-only priesthood, this tradition offers no guarantee of truth, "even if it has long been undisputed and taken for granted."[93] For Rahner, the fundamental question, therefore, is whether the notion of a "constant tradition" is a divine or merely a human tradition. The Congregation for the Doctrine of Faith would have Catholics believe that the notion of an all-male priesthood is of divine prescription, but there is nothing scripturally that clearly defines any

90. Ibid., 37.
91. Ibid., 39.
92. Ibid., 35.
93. Ibid., 38.

mandate of Christ that the priesthood is and will always be male only. Thus Rahner says, "there has been scarcely any reflection on the precise nature of this tradition in actual practice."[94] This is a point for Rahner that should involve much investigation rather than mere speculation, since many traditions have been known to be changed, modified, and broken.

In the second part of the *Declaration on the Question of the Admission of Women to the Ministerial Priesthood*, the Congregation for the Doctrine of Faith utilizes Scripture to support its position and says "the Attitude of Christ" was carefully examined, and it is well noted that Jesus did not call any woman to become part of the Twelve. Hence, Jesus intended, in principle, to exclude women from the priesty ministry for all times and under all sociological, historical, and theological conditions. Rahner rebuts this spurious allegation and says that "a purely historical exegesis of the texts from Scripture does not make the matter immediately obvious."[95] He claims that the Declaration does not consider the social and cultural aspects from the time of Christ and, therefore, assumes a false intention on the part of Jesus to bar women from the priesty ministry, which is not historically and sociologically sound.[96] Therefore, if Christ did not bring women to be a part of the Twelve, it was apparently because of the custom of the times and the attitudes towards women, for "it, very well, may have compromised his work and mission."[97]

According to the third section of the Declaration, on the practice of the Apostles, the Congregation for the Doctrine of Faith repeated the notion that in this matter, the apostles remained faithful to the attitude of Jesus. They went on to say that although Mary the mother of Jesus occupied a privileged place in the circle of those gathered in the upper room after the Lord's ascension (cf. Acts 1:14), it was not she who was called to the Twelve, but rather Matthias who took the place of Judas Iscariot.[98] So, Rahner argues, on the day of Pentecost, all were filled with the Holy Spirit, men and women together (cf. Acts 2:1–14). Yet the Congregation for the Doctrine of Faith contends that the proclamation of the fulfillment of the prophecies in Jesus' name was made only by "Peter and the eleven" (Acts

---

94. Ibid., 38.
95. Ibid., 36
96. Ibid., 38.
97. Our Lady's Warriors, "Commentary on the Declaration."
98. CDF, *Declaration on the Question*.

2:14).[99] There can be no question, Rahner claims, that Mary the mother of the incarnate Christ could have had any position that she desired. But it appears that Mary, in true humility, would not have upstaged the Apostles, for it was not the norm or custom of the time for women to take an active role in ministry. Jewish practice hardly permitted women to speak in the temple, let alone proclaim the Word of the Lord; and the Jewish mentality during that period did not accord great value to the witness of women, as is shown by Jewish custom and law.[100] On this slim basis, the Congregation for the Doctrine of Faith has concluded that the Apostles never thought of conferring ordination of women since they were convinced of their "male-only" duty of fidelity to the Lord on this point.[101]

In the fourth section of the Declaration, on the permanent value of the attitudes of Jesus and the Apostles, the Congregation for the Doctrine of Faith argues against the Church departing from the attitudes of Jesus and the Apostles, which they claim has been the tradition since the day of Pentecost.[102] To Rahner, if this attitude of the Congregation for the Doctrine of Faith prevails, all they have to do is to slightly modify their thinking process. However, to transform such thinking of the leadership is to convert the antiquated thinking of the hierarchy as exemplified in this document itself. The Congregation for the Doctrine of Faith seemed to have ignored the reality that this is a new age and women have been liberated and can contribute to the welfare of the Catholic Church. Women can bring a new dimension to the love of Christ and his ministry, while simultaneously bringing a renewed spirit to the Church, and especially to the altar of the Eucharist. This is something that seems to have been lacking for years.

In the fifth and final sections of the Declaration, the Congregation for the Doctrine of Faith offers additional defenses to their rigid views, and claims that the "Ministerial Priesthood in the Light of the Mystery of Christ" and the "Ministerial Priesthood Illustrated by the Mystery of the Church" have similarities with the first four sections of the Declaration. Rahner continues to argue that these reflections do not constitute a conclusive argument to the validity of the Declaration; he points out that the conclusions are apparent only to someone already convinced by the reasons

---

99. Ibid.
100. Our Lady's Warriors, "Commentary on the Declaration."
101. CDF, *Declaration on the Question.*
102. Ibid.

actually invoked, while such analysis only makes a very speculative impression on others.

In conclusion, therefore, the *Declaration on the Question of the Admission of Women to the Ministerial Priesthood* on the surface lacks credibility and seems slanted in the direction of conformity to the male-only brotherhood of priests; and it seems rather obvious that there is a hidden agenda on a deeper level that bars the ordination of women to the priesthood in the Catholic Church. Perhaps it relates to the deep-seated notion of discrimination, pride, sexism, fear of the unknown, and loss of control. The answer might be found in the notion of truth to those who truly believe that this is what Jesus really wanted. Only God knows the answer to this quandary. Whatever the reason, or lack thereof, women could certainly bring a new dimension to the priesthood and possibly alleviate the great burden of the shortage of priests that can minister to the faithful. Conceivably, the greatest possibilities that exists in the ordination of women to the priestly ministry is a renewed spirit of the faithful and the possibility of both genders loving and serving God at the eucharistic altar of Jesus Christ. This would be a new beginning for an old Church. For what can be lost as a Church? Look at the problems that the male-only clerics have caused the Church: scandals throughout the world, loss of vocations, lack of priests, closing of parishes, pedophile priests in the schools and parishes and other ministries, and bankruptcies of dioceses to settle unnecessary claims, etc. Is it possible that women might do a little better job in the priestly ministry? Consider the increase of credibility for starters, the potential increase at Sunday Mass and other services, the renewed spirit of the faithful laity, and a rehabilitated confidence in the leadership of the Vatican.

From an alternative perspective, Louis Gutiérrez suggests that the concept of male-only priests "is not of divine will"[103] and supports his thesis with biblical exegesis, doctrinal theology, moral, sacramental, liturgical, pastoral, nuptial, ecumenical, and mariological related texts. For example:He argues that, from a *biblical perspective*, "Only an uncritical 'fundamentalist' reading of certain passages of the New Testament can lead to the conclusion that the male-only priesthood is the normative will of the Lord." [104] Such readings and interpretations, he notes, violates the norm of good exegesis that is commonly accepted and practiced in the liturgical churches, including the Roman Catholic Church. For Gutiérrez,

---

103. Gutiérrez, "Perspectives on Canon 1024."
104. Ibid.

the biblical theory is centered in the notion that there are many texts in the New Testament, which suggest that the Church could be open to new possibilities on the issue of the ordination of women to the priesthood. For example, he cites, "the Eucharistic ecclesiology of John 6:35-58, which cannot be ignored." [105] Here he claims the Eucharist is the source and summit of all ecclesial life, for Jesus Christ is the bread of life in the Eucharist. And the love of Christ transcends all genders, male and female alike. [106] Thus if Christ transcends gender, then women may be ordained to the priesthood in the Roman Catholic Church.

From a *doctrinal perspective*, Gutiérrez views the notion of the male-only priesthood as a matter of discipline, not a matter of doctrine and still less a matter of faith. His argument is centered in the notion that the elevation of the male-only priesthood from a discipline to a doctrine is irrational, because such reasoning is based on a fundamentalist interpretation of certain passages of the New Testament that are insufficient in themselves to base such assumptions.[107]

Gutiérrez goes on to say that in the Creed we profess that the Church is apostolic, but not male-apostolic. To be an apostle or successor to the apostles, a person must take up the cause of Christ, and these individuals do not have to be from the male gender only. This line of reasoning becomes evident after the resurrection, when the risen Lord sent Mary Magdalene as "the apostle to the apostles." From a theological perspective, Gutiérrez proposes that "the male-only priesthood is not definable as divinely revealed truth."[108] And the male-only priesthood is not a matter of faith (*de fide*), for it only touches the expression of faith in an incidental way. Moreover, the encyclical "Ordinatio Sacerdotalis" was not issued infallibly, because the pope was not teaching *ex cathedra*, nor was he expressing the consensus of all the bishops in today's Church. Therefore, "the teaching that the Church is not authorized to ordain women is not infallible."[109]

From a *moral perspective*, Gutiérrez queries those who espouse the notion that women cannot be priests from the point of view that, if sexism and discrimination are rooted in evil, then why would Jesus exclude women from the twelve apostles? Was it because Jesus desired the apostles to be

---

105. Ibid.
106. Ibid.
107. Ibid.
108. Ibid.
109. Ibid.

all men? Maybe so . . . and then again, maybe not? Perhaps Jesus did not even consider it as a result of the concrete cultural condition that no longer exists in the civilized world.[110] But for sure, according to Scripture, women were not excluded from Jesus' discipleship. They were very much involved, and Scripture reveals that his choosing of only males to be apostles cannot be construed to exclude women from the possibility of ordination to the priesthood today.[111] Hence, the notion that females should be prohibited from the priesthood may be a misleading fallacy.

From a *sacramental perspective*, Gutiérrez contends that the celebration of the Eucharist requires an ordained priest to make the sacrament valid. No one can argue with this! But he qualifies this statement and observes that it is not the priest himself that makes this happen, but the power of God through the Holy Spirit in the miracle of transubstantiation. Thus God can create miracles through anyone, male or female alike, and it is not necessary that the priest who consecrates bread and wine at Mass be male. For Gutiérrez, "To act 'in persona Christi' is to act in the Second Person of the Most Holy Trinity, who assumed human nature as a male (a human limitation), but transcends gender as a Person."[112] The very idea, then, of an all-male priesthood by virtue of the fact that Jesus was male and the apostles were male is not of divine order.

From a *liturgical perspective*, Gutiérrez argues that men and women are mutually complementary with respect to the priesthood. But this does not mean that they are mutually exclusive, as in the case of all male priests, except for their purely physical dimensions.[113] He observes that is clearly experienced in the body language of conjugal love. For example, "the male's inclination is to love in order to allow himself to be loved."[114] Conversely, "the female allows herself to be loved in order to love in return." [115] This is the loving bond whereby male and female become one in the flesh, which is the union of man and women, a gift from God that parallels the communion between Christ and the Church, that is, the mutual self-surrender of the Church to Christ and Christ to the Church (Eph 5:31–32).

110. Ibid.
111. Ibid.
112. Ibid.
113. Ibid.
114. Ibid.
115. Ibid.

Further from a liturgical perspective, Gutiérrez posits that the unification and the key that unlocks the door to the priesthood for women parallel's the notion of the rain to the earth, sunshine to flowers, and Christ to his Church. Hence, in the ordination of women the Church will not be diminished, but rather enhanced and enriched through the body language of the liturgy, a language that should be the dialogue of the redeemed human body, as male is to female, fully healed and made one in partaking of the Eucharist, for this is God's will (John 6:56).[116] From this viewpoint, Gutiérrez observes, it is hard to see how the notion of the male-only priesthood can be understood and viewed as God's will, for it brings to the forefront a pattern of male domination that may only be rooted in pride, selfishness, sexism, and original sin (Gen 3:16). It has nothing to do with priests acting in the person of Jesus Christ in the Eucharist.

From the *ecumenical perspective*, Gutiérrez lays the foundation for this argument from the Anglican denomination, a community that supports ordination of women to the priestly ministry. He poses the question: in order to bridge the gap between the Catholic Church and other denominational confessions in the process of unification, is it therefore necessary to demand that the priestly vocation of women in the Anglican Communion be aborted? Then he answers his own question and says, "If so, would such nullification be for the glory of God and the good of souls? Or rather, are we excluding the Anglican Order from unity with Rome?"[117] Certainly, the elimination of women priests in the Anglican Communion would not be for the greater glory of God, nor would it achieve positive results for the good of souls and the sake of ecumenism. Such a demand to ask the Anglican Church to eliminate women from the priesthood would be preposterous. Therefore, from an ecumenical perspective, the ordination of women in the Christian world, and more particularly the Catholic Church, would not have a negative effect on unification, but rather act as a positive neutralizer in the quest for ecumenical unanimity.

Gutiérrez' final argument, from a *Marian perspective*, is a compilation of theories that include the notion that if Jesus wanted his mother to become a priest he would have made her one even though she was not one of the Twelve. Mary is the mother of Jesus Christ, the incarnate *Son of the Living God*. She already has a share in the priesthood of her Son and does not have to be ordained; she already is by virtue of her status: for *only corn*

---

116. Ibid.
117. Ibid.

can come from corn, only metal from metal, and only the blessed can come from the blessed. Nevertheless, according Gutiérrez, "I am utterly unable to see why Mary being the Mother of God means that other women cannot be priests of her Son."[118] The Christ-Mary mystery is the beginning of the mystical body of Christ, the Christ-Church relationship that will unfold until the Lord returns to divinize his Church. The ordination of women to the priesthood of Christ is "a continuation of the 'Assumption' along the way towards the new Jerusalem,"[119] a place where there is no more inequality, no more sexism, and no more male dominance, but rather a state of being where all are equal in the eyes of God and God's loving Son.

In sum, then, to Gutiérrez and many theologians in the Catholic tradition, women have a place and are needed in the priesthood of the Roman Catholic Church. Although such a development seems at times to be hopeless, "nothing is impossible for God" (Luke 1:37). The day of ordained woman "will come like a thief in the night" (Thess 5:2–4); it will come at a time when the faithful of both genders will respectfully take their positions at the communal altar of Jesus Christ.

Women Priests Today

While the Church fathers seem to ignore the signs of the age, a few fearless God-driven women have defied the notion of excommunication and founded an order of "Roman Catholic Womenpriests," an *international initiative of ordained womenpriests* within and yet outside the Roman Catholic Church. This order of womenpriests has rejected and disregarded the penalty of excommunication that was issued by the Vatican through the Congregation for the Doctrine of Faith on May 29, 2008, which stated that the "women priests and the bishops who ordained them would be excommunicated *latae sententiae*." These brave women of faith not only rejected the authority of the Congregation for the Doctrine of Faith, but they continued to do so in the face of fierce opposition from the hierarchy of the Catholic Church.[120] Their only response to Church leadership has been one of loyalty and service to the faithful. They are servants of the Lord Jesus Christ and "stand in the prophetic tradition of holy obedience to the Spirit's

118. Ibid.
119. Ibid.
120. Meehan, "Case for Women Priests." See the RCWP website at http://www.romancatholicwomenpriests.org.

call to change an unjust law that discriminates against women."[121] Theirs is a movement that is receiving enthusiastic responses from the faithful on all fronts of local, national, and international levels. The mission of womenpriests is to spiritually prepare, ordain, and support women and men from all states of life: those who are theologically qualified and committed to an inclusive model of the Roman Catholic Church. These ministers are centered in the response of Christ to "go, therefore and make disciples of all nations" (Matt 28:19). They are women and men dedicated to the call by the power of the Holy Spirit to minister to the faithful in the name of Christ.[122]

Edward Schillebeeckx observes that "presently, discontent in the Church is fieriest among women."[123] He goes on to say that it is no longer just discontent as a result of the negative experience within the institutional Church, but it is the attitude of indifference, discrimination, and sexism that has frustrated and driven women to form their own order of priests within the Church. Two thousand years ago, women and slaves were possessions of men, and therefore subject and less than equal to them in all things. These women are not just dissatisfied with the institutional Church but cognizant of the hierarchy's continued accusations and threats of excommunication. This intimidation has only made women all the more determined to achieve their goal, which is that of developing a "Women's Church" movement which intentionally accuses the patriarchal, masculine character of the Catholic Church and its leaders of unjustified discrimination.[124]

Womenpriests is an initiative within the Catholic Church that began with the ordination of seven women whose persistence and determination to serve the Lord appears radical—a term that was sometimes attributable to Jesus. Their mission is to reclaim the "ancient spiritual heritage" of Christ in "a more inclusive, Christ-centered, Spirit-empowered church of equals in the 21st century,"[125] a worthy goal for today and into the future, which most Christian communities should attempt to achieve. Some women bishops are, in fact, ordaining in full apostolic succession of new womenpriests to their order, a community that has been growing steadily throughout the United States and most of Western Europe. These devout Catholic Christians advocate the notion of a new model of priestly ministry united with

---

121. Ibid.
122. Ibid.
123. Schillebeeckx, *Church with a Human Face*, 236.
124. Ibid., 236–37.
125. Meehan, "Case for Women Priests."

followers with whom they serve and are deeply rooted in a response to Jesus who called both women and men to be disciples and equals while living, preaching, and teaching the gospel.[126] For as Jesus has said, "Anyone who is not against us is with us" (Mark 9:40). Hence, the Church can and should recognize these brave women as priests of Christ.

As a practical matter, how can anyone chastise these servants of the Lord? It seems that it may be better to engage and utilize the services of this community, rather than distance them from the Church's ultimate evangelical goals. Even the Pontifical Biblical Commission in 1976 concluded that there is no biblical reason for the Church to prohibit women from ordination. It was determined at the time that women and men were created equal in God's image, and both female and male may represent Christ as his priests.[127] For Jesus never ordained anyone—certainly not priests, deacons, presbyters, or even bishops. He never even mentioned the notion of ordaining priests in the Gospels. Jesus loved all his disciples, male and female alike. He also chose a woman to announce the good news to her entire village, and because of her testimony the people of the town accepted Jesus as the Messiah (John 4:6-42). So it is very possible that women may have a place in God's ministry of the priesthood. Surely, by the grace of God, the Catholic Church should open its heart to many of the issues that have been discussed here—proposals that are truly colored by the shades of modernity. From modern-day prophets like Rahner, Kelly, Metz, Gutiérrez, and Schillebeeckx as well as countless others, the eyes of the Catholic Church can be opened to new possibilities for positive change and renewal by enabling the Church to build a new, bigger, and stronger Catholic Christian Church. Then the Church that was built on the "rock of Peter" will return to its roots through the practice of love, forgiveness, understanding, and compassion to all, including those that are lost to contemporary Catholic Christianity.

In the following pages, we will explore the relationship of the Church to the poor, and the notion of "liberation theology," as related to the firsthand experience of Jon Sobrino, Gustavo Gutiérrez, and many others. We will also delve into the history of Dorothy Day, Archbishop Oskar Romero, and Reinhold Niebuhr, Christian leaders that have had a great impact on the Church's never-ending ministry to the poor, the abused, and those who suffer from injustice.

---

126. Ibid.
127. Ibid.

3 ───────────────────────────

Church Ministry to the Poor: A Beacon of Hope for the Future Church

ONE WONDERS . . . IF Jesus returned to earth in his original physical form what would he discover in the Church? Would he find that the Catholic Church of today resembles that of its origins: the *Church of the community of Jesus' followers* that was assembled by a group of disciples—those who worked hard, suffered much, and had little to offer God's people but *faith, hope, and love* in the message of a compassionate Savior? Or would the Lord perhaps see that his Church has evolved into something quite different, something on a grander scale? For example, an authoritative structured institution that seems to display, at times, inflexibility to innovative thinking, and a failure to adapt its practices and rules to the contemporary world? In any event, Jesus might be perplexed. For the Church of the present-day world exhibits very few of the characteristics that Jesus had inspired in his followers two thousand years ago.

In this connection, Karl Rahner has observed that ever since Vatican II, the Church that served the *poor*—sometimes known as the *Church of the poor*—has become a challenge for much of the hierarchy to emulate. For it is one thing to tell the world that one is a servant of Christ and that one's message is, therefore, believable, but it is quite another to live modestly and show the world, by example, that the church means what it says, and hence, that its message is credible.[1] For Rahner, the Church's deontological

---

1. Rahner, "Unreadiness of the Church's Membership to Accept Poverty," *TI* 14:270.

responsibility is to stand by the side of the poor, the oppressed, and those who struggle for daily existence.[2] The Church must exist as the catalyst that brings the rich and wealthy face to face with the compassion and suffering of Christ in order to fight against contemporary structures that favor a ruthless capitalism and a political imperialism that infects the world with its domineering selfishness, greed, and oppression.

The Church hierarchy, by all accounts of the Gospels, should never have given the appearance of having pursued wealth and riches. Such betrayal of its original calling only exacerbates the impression that the leaders of the Church catered to the rich and wealthy, while only the crumbs of its concerns fall from their table to those who truly hunger and thirst for justice. This widespread display of Church grandeur has sent the wrong message to the world, especially to those who struggle with deprivation and destitution. On the other hand, the Church leadership has been mandated by none other than Jesus Christ to set the example of true humility and altruistic service by practicing Jesus' own example of "servant leadership" (John 13: 17) to those who are less fortunate in their social standing.[3] The Church leaders have been called to pick up the cross of hunger and bear the banner of life for those that are truly poor and abused. "Otherwise," according to the liberation theologian Gustavo Gutiérrez, "their poverty means death."[4]

From this perspective, Karl Rahner asks whether the Church could ever be a credible witness to Christ's gospel message that is necessary to take part with the poor in their struggle against poverty.[5] Rahner claims that the problem for the Church is basically this: "a form of preaching which remains more or less socially ineffectual over a long period of time loses its credibility."[6] When the hierarchy preaches the same message year after year and decade after decade and is not supported with concrete action on behalf of the poor and disadvantaged, their discourse begins to lack the pastoral force needed for a church to accomplish believability. This parallels the Apostle James's declaration that "faith without works is dead" (Jas 2:20). The essence of integrity and trust, for a church, if not accompanied with positive action on behalf of a suffering people, eventually turns to empty words that fall on deafened ears. As a result, people become disillusioned. When the Church's nice-sounding

---

2. Ibid., 270.
3. Ibid., 270.
4. Gutiérrez, *We Drink from Our Own Wells*, 9.
5. Rahner, "Unreadiness of the Church's Membership," *TI* 14:272.
6. Ibid., 272.

words are not accompanied by positive courageous action, this in turn leads to a vicious circle of disbelief in church credibility.[7]

The Church preaches that people of faith must eliminate poverty, hunger, and abuse throughout the world. But the question arises whether the Church itself does anything really positive to eliminate the root cause of injustice, other than a token gift to the poor and the hungry. In the opinion of Rahner, the Church's prophetic message can become more or less ineffectual, and the effectiveness of its preaching can render its message "unworthy of belief."[8] Sooner or later the discourse turns to ecclesiastical spin and destined to become shallow and repetitious whenever the leadership does not practice what it preaches. It then would seem that the Church has followed the old cliché, "Do as I say, not as I do." And for this very reason, Rahner claims that the Church is in danger of becoming rich, and it desires to stay that way.[9] He goes on to say:

> Those within the Church who set the standards, the pope, the bishops, and the priests, themselves have levels of living which are too high in the advanced countries. They fail to achieve any really firm social awareness. They prefer to adhere to the rich, to the establishment in the capitalist and imperialist countries, and so on.[10]

It is easy to understand that, in their ecclesiastical life, some of the clerics enjoy a certain level of comfort in *the good life. They* hardly have any desire to live in squalor or poverty. Perhaps some take the attitude that says, "Let others take care of the poor and those less fortunate. I have the comfort I need and do not want to part with it; after all, we live a celibate life and deserve to live well." This outlook may be so, but this is not the gospel message or the mission that Christ undertook. "Even today," Rahner laments, "we are still setting up monuments to the prophets in order to avoid having to obey what they preached."[11]

According to Rahner, the Church leadership should take the lead in setting the example in how to live modestly and serve others in need.[12] Church leaders should exemplify the life of Jesus and live in humility that lets their light shine before the world (Matt 5:14–16). Only in this way can

---

7. Ibid., 272.
8. Ibid., 272–73.
9. Ibid., 273.
10. Ibid., 273–74
11. Ibid., 276
12. Ibid., 273.

their preaching about the poor and those in need become meaningful and believable. It seems to be true that people tend to follow leaders who lead by example and not just in word alone. But this for Rahner is only part of the Church's social problem, which brings us to the simple question: "Will it be possible for the Church (in particular the clergy) to mobilize the laity in this resolve and struggle against poverty in the world?"[13] In Rahner's view, overcoming world poverty should be a joint effort of both the clergy and the laity. For poverty is a wretched condition that can and must be stamped out by all Christians. However, Rahner argues further that "the Church will not succeed in leading the struggle against poverty by means of its own 'poverty,' even though in itself it has a duty to do this."[14] To Rahner, the leadership of the Church, it seems, will not in any adequate sense succeed in mobilizing the clerics and laity in the effort to eliminate poverty in the world unless, in the Church, there is a readiness of the clergy to accept poverty and undertake to modify their comfortable means of living in order to exemplify Christ's life for the poor.

The purpose behind Rahner's argument is that if we seriously study the history of the Church and evaluate its teaching, we will find that it is basically a Church of *sinners*. This truth helps people to understand that it is impossible from the outset why the Church appears capable of failing its major historical mission as it has done so many times in the past.[15] Failure time and again has *de facto* plagued the Church with its inefficiencies and poor judgments. One can cite, for example, the case of its confrontation with the cultures of Eastern Asia and the dispute on adapting to Eastern Asian cultural rites. Has the Church adequately "coped" in any positive sense with the Enlightenment? Has it managed to reject the movement toward church-state segregation at the right time? Is it not through its own fault that it has, in large measure, lost the "poor working class" in many countries of the world?[16] Even in smaller matters, to this very day its blunders persist. One glaring example is when Pope Benedict XVI lifted the excommunication of British Bishop Richard Williamson, who then publicly denied the Holocaust in statements that were an embarrassment to the papacy. The pope had no knowledge of the bishop's position and was

13. Ibid., 274.
14. Ibid., 274.
15. Ibid., 274.
16. Ibid., 275.

deluged with bad press from the Jewish world about the incident.[17] What about the recent attempt by the Irish Catholic Church to cover up and thwart the release of the Ryan Report, the comprehensive account of widespread priestly abuses—sexual and physical—of thousands of youngsters under the care of the Catholic Church of Ireland? This is a crime against humanity that will cost the Church more than the hundreds of millions of dollars it has committed to settle these cases.

"Yet the fact remains," says Rahner, "even in the Church despite its existence, historical faults of the greatest magnitude are possible."[18] He goes on to say that ecclesiologists should look into the crises of the Church and attempt to address the problems that Church leaders have caused. There are continuing crises that are far from being adequately explored at the theological level, even though, in Rahner's view, "there are enough people nowadays who regard the Church as discredited . . . to such an extent that for them it has become totally unworthy of belief in its claim to have been founded by God."[19]

For Rahner, when it comes to the subject of poverty, the Church has failed to live up to its promise, namely, the concern of Jesus Christ for the poor. World poverty appears to be far from the hierarchy's mind; they have made little concerted effort to cure or eliminate the condition of poverty other than by appealing to secular means. In other words, the Church accepts scarcely any effective responsibility for the poor other than its sanctimonious rhetoric, which has often been its practice. This lack of responsibility prompts Rahner to conclude:

> The Church will act more or less in exactly the same way as a secular society, perhaps very slightly better, but by and large just the same. We see and yet we do not see, we will and yet we do not will, we do something and it is too little. Our un-readiness to accept poverty remains.[20]

Rahner has realized that societal change and modernization have developed far too slowly to allow a more effective Church action for the poor in the foreseeable future. This ineffectiveness itself constitutes a crisis. It seems inconceivable that, in a so-called modern age, hunger still exists

---

17. Associated Press, "Pope Didn't Know."
18. Rahner, "Unreadiness of the Church's Membership," *TI* 14:276.
19. Ibid., 277.
20. Ibid., 277.

in the world—a fact that looms over the richest Church in the world. Too many wealthy nations and their churches seem ineffective in alleviating the suffering of the many poor in this troubled world.[21] Churches resort too often to the mere preaching against poverty while doing little to alleviate the plight of the poor. Its inactions are akin to the "cheap grace" excoriated by Dietrich Bonhoeffer. According to Bonhoeffer, "cheap grace is preaching forgiveness without repentance, baptism without the discipline of community, the Lord's Supper without confession of sin, grace without discipleship, grace without the cross, and grace without the living incarnate Jesus Christ."[22] This cheapened grace should also include preaching the elimination of poverty without any Church-driven responsibility to combat its existence effectively. Because the Catholic Church ranks unquestionably among the richest and most influential churches in the world, it should undertake the greatest responsibility of all to drive the "demons of destitution" from the world of the poor. This is a mission that can be conjoined to the responsibility of rich nations to assist the poorer nations of the world.

For example, in 1961, by executive order President John F. Kennedy established the Peace Corps, an assembly of young people who would volunteer to serve others less fortunate for a period of two years. The object of their mission was to help improve social conditions in the poorer nations of the world through such programs as agricultural techniques, mathematics, science, vocational training, business, public administration, and education in literacy, which can help the people to develop their own natural resources. Young adults at that time gravitated to the cause and contributed their time and hard work in a concerted effort to alleviate some of life's burdens for the impoverished in forgotten places of the world.[23] The question then becomes: can the Roman Catholic Church emulate the Peace Corps by creating an organization of clerics and laity to seek out and undertake a sincere attempt to eliminate world hunger and poverty in developing nations? If creative thought, insight, and some capital were invested, it is quite possible that the Church could implement a plan to organize hundreds, if not thousands, of young people and clerics to overcome the devastations of poverty in countries where the Church can be at work in caring for the poor and those abused by the ravages of a heartless culture. It is quite possible that the Church could take a proactive role in eliminating once and

21. Kelly and Nelson, *Cost of Moral Leadership*, 132.
22. Ibid., 132.
23. Wikipedia, "Peace Corps."

for all, or at least significantly reducing, deaths caused by poverty. This idea might create such excitement in the Church that young people might enthusiastically be drawn to such a worthy cause. And the Catholic Church may gain a few converts in the effort.

Unfortunately, Rahner claims that the Roman Catholic Church will not succeed in organizing such a program so long as there is unreadiness in the Church to enter fully into the struggle against poverty by setting an example for the world to see that it means what it preaches. One way that the Church may be able to accomplish this goal is to embrace poverty in its own lifestyle as a condition for eliminating poverty in the world.[24] In the end, no genuine Christian should be able to say with any degree of integrity that he simply is going along with the herd in matters concerning the poor. All Christians, especially clerics of the Church, have a responsibility to battle the evils caused by poverty and its systematic injustice and devastating effects. Quite often, Catholic missionaries, in the self-sacrificing poverty they embrace, have set the example for the leadership of the Church that live lavishly and are settled in the more comfortable zone of their clerical residences; they should emulate with amazing benefit, for Church credibility, solidarity with the poor.

Portrait of Poverty in the Context of Church Credibility

The contemporary portrait of poverty for the Catholic Church is not attractive. The visible experiences of the truly poor, the distressed, and the hungry are social conditions that are repugnant to the average observer. It gives one the sickening feeling that the image of the poor is weary. People like Mother Theresa, Francis of Assisi, Archbishop Oscar Romero, Dorothy Day, Reinhold Niebuhr, Karl Rahner, Gustavo Gutiérrez, and many others have understood and known the social circumstances of the impoverished very well. But where do those in power stand on this issue—people like the pope, the bishops, and the clergy, including those who constitute the laity of the Church? What are they actually doing to eradicate this ever-growing problem of poverty on planet Earth? Not in a token way, with the crumbs that fall from the table of plenty, but with a positive activist approach that is supported with prayer, and reinforced by concerted action on the part of church leaders of all denominations.

---

24. Rahner, "Unreadiness of the Church's Membership," *TI* 14:278.

Those who live in the condition of poverty exist in a state of being that embraces the lack of essentials for the sustenance of a fully dignified life. Their social condition is that which too often breeds hunger, sickness, utter despair, and death. We see it surface in places where the hungry and the impoverished suffer from the need to sustain decent lives. Assuredly, poverty can stifle the spirit and rob the soul of ambition. For those who bear this burden, it is a circumstance that is nearly impossible to rise from without supported help from the world. Through compassionate persons of means and institutions dedicated to helping the poor, poverty has become akin to a disease that suppresses the talent and hope of countless millions who otherwise may contribute something of value to the benefit of others. This "disease" has been recognized by the World Bank in the following report:

> Poverty is hunger, lack of suitable shelter, and sickness while not being able to afford a doctor. It is not having access to education nor knowing how to read. It is not having a job, fear of the future, and meagerly living one day at a time. Poverty is powerlessness, lack of representation and restricted freedom. And lastly, it is losing a child to illness brought about by filth, unclean sanitation, and impure water.[25]

Sadly, each day approximately eighteen thousand children throughout the world die due to poverty. Given the affluence of so many nations, most of these deaths occur in South Asia and Sub-Saharan Africa.[26] This tragedy is inexcusable. According to the United Nations International Children's Emergency Fund (UNICEF), these children die silently from hunger and sickness in some of the poorest villages on earth in places where only the few visit. They are far removed from the scrutiny and the conscience of the world and the Church. Being poor and weak in life makes these dying multitudes even more invisible in death. It is well documented that eight hundred million people residing in underdeveloped countries of the world are poor, undernourished, and in need of assistance.[27] These unfortunates lack the ability to rise from their impoverished circumstances, or to know they still belong as the children of God, worthy of climbing up from the depths of their circumstances. They are the *voiceless*, desperately in need of a prophetic herald bearing their plight and call for help. According to former UN Secretary General Kofi Annan, "Almost half the world's popu-

25. World Bank, "Poverty Overview."
26. Shah, "Poverty Facts and Stats."
27. Ibid.

lation lives on less than two dollars a day; yet even this statistic fails to capture the humiliation, powerlessness and brutal hardship that is the daily lot of the world's poor."[28] Surely, poverty destroys the hopes and dreams of those who suffer from this affliction. The poor and destitute go through life with their inner music and God-given endowments stifled like a candle that is prematurely extinguished.

Leonardo Boff has observed that poverty carries with it the devastation that prevents the poor from developing their God given abilities. He argues that poverty destroys the emotional life of those who suffer its abuse and alienates people's relationship with others. Poverty, he says, continually places obstacles in the way of the essential vocation of human beings to develop and expand their God-given talents and abilities beyond mere survival. It leads the poor to envy, hatred, and violence against those responsible for their misery, and very often they end up blaming God or religion for their meager existence by raising their fist against heaven.[29]

In Latin America, another prophetic Church figure, Gustavo Gutiérrez, considered the father of "liberation theology," asserts that the circumstances surrounding the poor and the abused must be confronted. Understanding poverty, he contends, is no longer an unknown disease from the past. He observes that now people know and recognize the ravages of poverty and that its tentacles sink deeply into the heart of the poor. Gutiérrez goes on to say that there were times when we thought we knew the root cause of this evil, what it is that keeps the poor from living a modest life, but that is no longer the case. Poverty today is simply not the misfortune or the whims of the universe; rather, it is a social injustice to those who are poor and abused by the wealthy powerful establishments who, at times, would exploit them for the sake of profits and ill-gotten gain.[30] In Central and South America and other Latin nations, it reflects the extrapolation of an extremely old yet simple equation: *the rich get richer and the poor get poorer.* For Gutiérrez, the first step in alleviating the problem of poverty and social injustice for the poor is "for the Church to proclaim a new epoch."[31] This is the time for renewal in the Church by updating its thinking on social justice and the acknowledgment of formerly ignored or even scorned traditions concerning the poor, particularly in the area of social justice services. Therefore, the

---

28. Ibid.
29. Boff, *Saint Francis*, 206.
30. James, "Wisdom of Gustavo Gutierrez."
31. Nickoloff, "Introduction," in Gutierrez, *Essential Writings*, 18.

Church must take the lead in this mission and become proactive when it comes to addressing the difficult challenges of poverty in the world.[32]

Gutiérrez's "theology of liberation" parallel's the biblical struggles as described in Exodus, the prophetic writings, and the New Testament Gospels. In truth, his theological, political, and spiritual reflections are at the heart of the "mystery of love," which is the mystery of God for those who are poor, oppressed, and destitute. He insists, "It cannot be otherwise."[33] Gutiérrez argues that to call oneself a follower of Christ has meaning only to those who actively partake in the struggle for freedom from exploitation of the poor in Latin America and other parts of the world where poverty and abuse has become a way of life.[34] Living a genuine spiritual life centered on helping the poor is a way of loving and practicing the example of Christ in solidarity with all human beings. To Gutiérrez, it is releasing people from the chains of worldly cravings and redirecting that desire to the care of our sisters and brothers in serious need. It is what he deems the "spirituality of liberation": a movement towards freedom for those who are oppressed, exploited, and poor—more particularly, the masses who live a life of misery in Latin America and underdeveloped countries, beneath the yoke of the rich and wealthy who hold the levers of economic power in a world where the poor abound. Gutiérrez insists that the Church's espousal of a mission to the poor from oppression is where the Spirit of the Lord exists (2 Cor 3:17).[35] He puts forth the related notion that the spirituality of liberation must be preceded by a *conversion* to serve the Lord. This is the radical transformation of oneself through *thinking, feeling, and loving* others as Jesus taught and practiced in the Gospels. Following the message and mission of Christ initiates the spiritual conversion and commitment to those in need in the process of liberating the poor, the oppressed, and all those who suffer injustice. Gutiérrez points out that "the evangelical conversion is the touchstone of all spirituality."[36] This is the interior commitment that transforms minds and hearts, which is required to change the world and the Church itself by caring, in Jesus' name, for the poor. According to Gutiérrez, evangelical conversion is, however, only the first step in the process of meaningful change in the Church. He maintains that

---

32. Ibid., 18.
33. Gutierrez, *Essential Writings*, 56.
34. Gutierrez, *Essential Writings*, 56.
35. Gutierrez, *Essential Writings*, 287.
36. Gutierrez, *Essential Writings*, 288.

the spirituality of liberation must be followed by the living sense of *gratuitousness*: the grateful bonding with the Lord that binds one to all human kind. It becomes the threshold to freedom and the gateway to liberty. More than anything else, such gratuitousness is a gift from God that is far from being passive, but rather, demands active vigilance. As Saint Paul counsels all Christians, "Offer yourselves to God as men who have come back from the dead to life and your bodies to God as weapons for justice" (Rom 6:13). More than anything else, Gutiérrez supports the notion that prayer is the channel to gratuitousness in God's service. Praying fervently to God leads to freeing oneself from religious alienation; it is to bond with the presence of the *Holy*. Prayer strips us from the egocentric center, universalizes one's love for others, and opens the heart to be gratuitous to all. For how is it possible to pray with one's whole heart and one's whole soul and not love and care for one's sisters and brothers in need?[37] When Gutiérrez speaks of those who are impoverished, his belief is centered on the unfortunate individuals who lack the basic essentials of existence, those who are without the economic goods necessary for human life worthy of its name, conditions that must be rejected by all people in all corners of the world. In his far-reaching analysis, he notes that "In Christian circles, occasionally there is a tendency to give material poverty a positive meaning and to see it almost as a human and religious ideal. It is sometimes seen as an ideal of austerity and indifference to the things of this world and the precondition for a life in conformity with the Gospel."[38] However, there is no virtue in poverty unless one makes a conscious lucid decision to be poor, materially, for the sake of the gospel by serving others in need, such as Saint Francis of Assisi, Mother Theresa, and many others have done for the sake of Christ. Hence, liberation theology is the focus of millions of people who suffer from a life of oppression and the lack of the basic necessities of life. This is the poverty of Jesus Christ as embraced by many Catholic liberation activists. Thus, the contemporary Church, through these exemplary Catholics, should recognize more fully its responsibilities to the poor and make the "evangelical conversion" to take the necessary action to address more effectively the dilemma of the poor, the abused, and the oppressed. This dedication to the destitute will enabled the Church to survive. It can no longer afford to pontificate to the rich and the wealthy aristocrats, while fighting the so-called "safe issues" like abortion and same-sex marriage. The Church's primary

---

37. Gutierrez, *Essential Writings*, 289.
38. Gutierrez, *Essential Writings*, 292.

concern must be to the poor and those who are abused in the hills, towns, and roads of Latin America, Central Africa, and other parts of the world. In this outreach to those in need lies the message and mission of Christ.

Liberation theologian Jon Sobrino, from El Salvador, takes the more critical approach and argues that "the Church does not understand its mission, as bringing the people down from the cross."[39] He has observed that seeing the Church from within, as a Jesuit, it appears to look like a scattering of movements rather than a compact body determined to alleviate the struggles of the poor and abused. It has signs that are more like places of easy, infantilizing comfort, as opposed to reasoned and committed faith. For Sobrino,

> The Church of today appears to be sleeping. It no longer hears the voice of the poor majorities, but listens instead to its traditional constituency the people who attend worship. The Church, it seems, is preoccupied with itself. It seeks to regain positions of cultural, political, and even economic power. It does not lack for clients, because the neo-liberal model has increased the anguish, the despair, the insecurity, and the bewilderment of the people.

For him, "the Church is in need of change and conversion."[40] However difficult and embarrassing this statement of Sobrino must be to the hierarchy of the Catholic Church, the truth must be spoken with deference to the poor, the unfortunate, and those who have no voice in the world. Except for the tokenism that the poor receives from the Church, which are the crumbs that fall from the tables of the rich, it offers very little hope of recovery from the pain of poverty. For the Church that has invoked an image of itself in which all are supposedly equal, it ends up too often being a Church of the few, which is the rich, the affluent, and the powerful.

In this connection, Karl Rahner has warned that the prospects are high that the Church will continue its meager level of community support for the poor in underdeveloped countries. If the Church's maneuvers are half-hearted, he notes, its efforts will only serve to evade the main problems of poverty and not offer effective relief to those under the burden of scarcity. In this event, the affluent churches will only alleviate their conscience. And this, to Rahner, will be the course of action that the Church as well as the affluent in secular society will have taken. It seems that few really care to take the lead in the process of overcoming the problem of poverty. For Rahner, "nothing

---

39. Sobrino, *Witnesses to the Kingdom*, 137.
40. Ibid., 136.

more can be expected in practice even from those who are forced to accept what is, by our standards, a more modest way of life, any more than it is from the rich and prosperous; for no one among us likes to pay enough for a banana to ensure that the banana picker can be given a really just reward for his labor."[41] According to Rahner, all Christians are responsible, even in a small way, for the care of the poor, the abused, and the oppressed. The student who is opposed to "imperialism and capitalism" still finds the means to take a leisurely vacation and enjoy the good things life offers; and the professor of theology finds nothing wrong with living in a house of his own, and perhaps a summer getaway also while in pursuit of his "profound studies." Rahner contends that people of faith belong to a "Church of sinners," and therefore are accountable for their actions or inactions by the way they live according to the gospel of Jesus. Moreover, the greatest responsibility for the care of the poor, the abused, and the distraught lie in the heart of those who publicly profess the Word, namely, the clerics who claim to hold the authority of none other than Jesus Christ himself.

A few years ago, during a Good Friday homily, Pope Benedict XVI proclaimed, "In the mirror of the cross, we have seen all the suffering of humanity today. We saw the suffering of abandoned abused babies, threats against families, the division in the world in the pride of the rich and the misery of all those who suffer, hunger, and thirst. Surely God is deeply pained." This papal statement represents a positive movement in the direction of the Church to help the poor, the suffering, and the abused in the world. The message is a call for hope and dedication in the true spirit of the gospel. Nonetheless, mere words without action to alleviate conditions of poverty and injustice that is so devastating in the modern world are not enough to move a molehill of the rich let alone the mountain of poverty for the poor. The truth must be shouted from the hilltops with more intensity than the magnitude of the evils faced by the hungry; it must be spoken by those in authority as though Jesus Christ has said it himself. Then, finally, the Word of Christ must be backed with positive practical plans to eradicate ultimately the devastating condition of poverty, a course of action that should be based on courage and determination in the face of attacks and persecution on the Church leaders. Surely, the Church can only grow and become stronger in the face of adversity. It is hoped that the pontiffs' homily will have real meaning for the Church's mission to the poor.

---

41. Rahner, "Unreadiness of the Church's Membership," *TI* 14:278.

Those Who Live the Message of Hope for the Church of the Poor: The Example of Dorothy Day

In the life and work of Dorothy Day lies a spirited soul that followed the "still small voice within." Dorothy was an advocate of the poor, the hungry, and the homeless in the heart of the Great Depression. She was not someone that just talked about the poor and homeless. She was a hands-on person that was actively involved in feeding and aiding the poor and destitute. If one were to summarize the character of Dorothy Day, it would have to reflect the real meaning behind Psalm 27.3: "Though an army encamps against me, my heart will not fear." Dorothy placed complete faith and trusts in the Lord and practiced her spiritual mandate to "Let go and let God be God."

Filled with courage and inner strength, Dorothy was a tenacious fighter for the hungry and the homeless sisters and brothers of Jesus. If this "reformed sinner" did not know the scriptural verses of the New Testament, such would not matter. Dorothy lived the gospel through love, understanding, and compassion for others, faithfully serving Jesus Christ by feeding and caring for the poor, the hungry, the lowly, and even the prostitutes and the mentally imbalanced—all those not able to lift themselves up in any meaningful way. This very simple lady was filled with faith, hope, and trust in the gospel of Jesus for the sake of others less fortunate. Whether she was aware of it or not, the Lord was surely guiding her through the dark days of the greatest economic crisis in the history of America. She had no doubt it was Jesus that summoned her, a modern-day sinner-turned-saint, to "Feed my sheep" (John 21:7).

After going through an unfortunate love affair, surviving an abortion, and living with a man as a common-law husband only to leave him and become a Catholic, one could hardly call her struggle a spiritual journey with Christ.[42] But Dorothy's call from the Lord came in a strange way. It started one evening when a French emigrant and activist, Peter Maurin, who fancied himself a "troubadour of God," knocked on the door to her apartment. During the course of their conversation, he planted a seed of challenge in her heart that grew in abundance in strange and unpredictable ways. Her journey led to the creation of a newspaper known as *The Catholic Worker*, a shelter for the homeless, bread for the hungry, and a farming commune where people could work, eat, and enjoy the fruits of their labor, thereby

---

42. Day, *Long Loneliness*, 132–33.

restoring pride in "self-reliance." But Dorothy was convinced it was Jesus who nurtured that seed with divine guidance and love in the call to serve others.[43] In *The Road Less Traveled*, M. Scott Peck claims that "Life is difficult," and it is for many, especially as it was in the 1930s. But being among those who endured that difficult period in American history, life was not just difficult—it was nearly impossible. My father, Peter J. Calvanese, once told me, "Back then son, I picked up coal that fell to the ground from the railroad cars just to have a little heat in the dead of winter."

For Dorothy Day, life was just not difficult, but nearly impossible; but through the grace of God and faith in Christ, she managed to keep it all together through struggle and adverse conditions. Not even the Catholic Church's officialdom or Catholic Charities gave her a helping hand. But Dorothy was unafraid of the difficulties she suffered. Her attitude was that of a positivist, a messenger of hope for a renewal of Church credibility, and a lioness and fearless warrior for Christ. As she proclaimed:

> We are not the Church, we are not Catholic Charities, and we are not the state in which we turn for help at times. Cardinal Spellman didn't ask me to take on this job, nor did the Mayor of New York. It just happened. It is the living from day to day, with faith in the living Christ, taking no thought for the morrow, and seeing Jesus in all who come to us, and trying literally, to live and follow the gospel.[44]

It was not false pride or stubbornness that kept her from seeking help from organized religion or the public bureaucracy. Dorothy did not talk about the poor. She never asked, "What should we do?" or said, "Let's pray for the hungry." Rather, she lived the message of the gospel by following the Sermon on the Mount: "Give to him who asks; love your enemies, feed the hungry, do good to those who hate you, pray for those who persecute you" (Matt 5:44). For Dorothy Day, these are the "works of mercy" and the only way for any Christian church to be that calls itself a follower of Jesus Christ. Dorothy raised most of her revenues that she used to help the poor through donations from those who were interested and able to help. She was a strong-willed person who did not beg for anything, but somehow, through faith in the power of prayer to solve problems and difficulties, troubles just seemed to work out. Her work managed to survive and even succeed in helping the poor. For example, at one point in time her checking account was two hundred dollars overdrawn—a very large sum in 1930.

43. Day, *Loaves and Fishes*, 7.
44. Ibid., 8.

On her way back from the print shop, she stopped in at a local church and said a prayer to Saint Joseph the Worker for help and guidance. By the time she returned home a woman had made a donation in the exact amount of the overdraft.[45] Coincidence . . . possibly? Maybe the power of prayer instead? Dorothy Day intuitively believed, "We pray for the help we need, and it comes."[46] Dorothy felt that when people give with a caring heart this very act of giving impresses on the giver the feeling of self-fulfillment; it is the liberating feeling one receives through kindness, compassion, and love toward others in need. When one opens her heart to the poor, the unfortunate, and those who are drowning in the abyss of poverty, one exhibits the greatest resistance to the problem of systemic evil. This is the difference between calling oneself a Christian and being Christ-like. It is leaving one's comforts behind and getting the job done for the love of Jesus in the person of his poor and hungry children. For Dorothy, the greatest challenge of all was to learn how to effectuate a revolution of the heart. This is the transformation that begins with the conscious decision to change the world for the better, something the Church and laity together can effectively achieve by loving and caring for all sisters and brothers without the necessities of life.

Recently, in Rome there was speculation over Dorothy's canonization. Whether or not she is publicly recognized as a saint is not important. She already has been acclaimed sainthood by the people she has helped. But what is truly important to know and understand as Christians is the call to emulate the work of this great lady, even in a small way, to help lessen the pain, the suffering, and the hunger of those that are less fortunate and plagued with poverty. For most Catholics are not called to be like Dorothy Day . . . nevertheless, all are called to be Christ-like.

The Example of Archbishop Oscar Romero

Another uncanonized saint that represents the Catholic Church leadership at its best and lived the message of the gospel of Christ is Archbishop Oscar Romero. Prior to his assignment to lead the dioceses of San Salvador, his reputation was that of a bookish conservative, a traditionalist that lacked the courage for change. Romero was a conservative cleric that did not look for trouble. This stereotypic role of "minister to the flock" was just what Rome preferred in El Salvador—someone the Vatican could control, a

---

45. Ibid., 191.
46. Ibid., 188.

leader who could keep peace with the government and mind the spiritual business of the Church without alienating or infuriating anyone in authority. So Romero was their man.

Archbishop Romero made a sincere attempt to walk the *straight and narrow* by following the dictates of his superiors and the strict canonical rules pertaining to office. According to Jon Sobrino, he had been very much under the influence of *Opus Dei*, an ultra-conservative organization of laity and secular priests under the governance of a prelate appointed by the pope.[47] However, after arriving in San Salvador as the primate archbishop, his life would never be the same. Within hours of his arrival, Archbishop Romero was informed of the murder of Jesuit priest Father Rutilio Grande, SJ, and two peasant civilians, a young boy, and an old man. Sobrino reports that his face was grim and his demeanor revealed that of deep disappointment. Sobrino goes on to say that here was an ecclesial leader at the beginning of his newly appointed archiepiscopal ministry not able to celebrate with joy as he should; rather, he was awash in arrests and torture, and now suddenly the assassination of an elderly peasant, a young boy, and a Jesuit priest. To say the least, he was shaken in the first few days of his reign.[48]

During the months that followed, Archbishop Romero gradually seemed to change. He actually asked the Jesuit community for their input and help, where previously he had kept his distance. Most of the Catholic Church hierarchy was under the false assumption that the Jesuits in Latin America were under the influence of Marxist ideology, and that was forbidden by the conservatives in Rome. But these thoughts and impressions, systematically, appeared to dwindle in the mind of Romero as he came to understand and know that the Jesuit community sincerely desired to help the poor and the oppressed of San Salvador. After much prayer and discussion, Archbishop Romero came to the conclusion that in order to be an effective minister to the people, it was incumbent to stand up to the rich, powerful, oligarchic government that was in control of the country.[49] According to Sobrino, "Archbishop Romero had felt what St. Ignatius Loyola sensed in his contemplation on societal sin, when in the eyes of his imagination he stood before Christ crucified and asked himself this question: 'What will I do for Christ?'"[50] In those moments of reflection, Sobrino

---

47. Wikipedia, "Opus Dei."
48. Sobrino, *Witnesses to the Kingdom*, 12.
49. Ibid., 15.
50. Ibid., 18.

notes that Archbishop Romero was gradually transformed. Father Rutilio's death was the impetus that provided the thrust for Romero to change and the newness in the direction of his thinking that became a most important center in his life and ministry. This transformative experience was amongst what the Latin clerics came to know as "Rutilio's miracle,"[51] which certainly had an impact on Romero's attitude to liberalize his heart toward the suffering peasants of El Salvador.

The second factor in Romero's transformation, as El Salvador's hierarchical leader, was the idea that prior to his arrival most of the clerics in San Salvador were uncomfortable with his appointment, since he was so conservative and opposed to the idea of liberation theology in the spirit of Medellin. The 1968 synod at Medellin, Columbia, where the Latin American bishops had decided to change their agenda to: "The Church in the Present Day Transformation of Latin America in Light of the Council," a program that had infuriated the Vatican. The bishops' main theme at the synod was: peace, justice, education, and the elimination of poverty. It was the beginning of the transformation of the Latin American Church and the changes that were necessary in keeping with the message of Jesus Christ. The city of Medellin, therefore, had become the symbol of hope and renewal for the Latin American bishops.[52] As a conservative, Archbishop Romero was originally opposed to the synod at Medellin. However, in light of his new transformation, those he thought were conservatives turned against him and provided no support for his change of heart. On the other hand, those who sustained the spirit of Medellin became his strongest liberal advocates. These were the only clerics that were behind him, those that bolstered his spirit when he needed it most. This newfound support reinforced his feelings of change and transformation.[53]

But the third and final factor in Archbishop Romero's conversion—which was the definitive factor and the one that kept him faithful to the will of God to the very end—was the people of San Salvador: the poor, the abused, and those who suffered indignities. It was the peasants and their families from the towns and villages who always gave him their greatest respect, acceptance, support, affection, and love who were mostly responsible for the change in the Archbishop's heart and soul. These were Romero's people. In Sobrino's words:

51. Ibid., 18.
52. Brown, *Gustavo Gutiérrez*, 11.
53. Sobrino, *Witnesses to the Kingdom*, 18.

> But the poor certainly hoped for an archbishop such as he proved to be. And the fact is, as I have already remarked, that in El Salvador, as in so many other places in Latin America, before the Church made an option for the poor, the poor had made an option for the Church. They had found no one else to defend them, not in the government, not in the armed forces, not in the political parties, and not in private enterprise. For Archbishop Romero took them into his heart, and they were there to stay.[54]

Archbishop Romero was certainly the man for the poor and the oppressed in El Salvador. Sobrino observes that the poor must have found in him what the prophet Isaiah contemplated in the "Suffering Servant of Yahweh," and as St. Paul saw in the crucified Christ: light and salvation to the oppressed. For indeed that is what he was—a beacon of light to the hopeless and a herald of salvation to the voiceless. Archbishop Romero was someone who saw and felt the anguish caused by the evildoers of society and set out to make it right in spite of the oppositions of the government and the military authority who threatened his very existence. After living the life as an ultra-conservative Catholic cleric, at age fifty-nine Archbishop Romero saw the light of salvation in the poor and the oppressed in San Salvador. Not only did he undertake a conversion of heart, but in the darkness of personal degradation, at the hands of the rich and the military, he found a new experience of God. Sobrino writes, "Never again would he be capable of separating God from the poor, or his faith in God from his defense of the poor."[55] Then, on March 24, 1980, while celebrating Mass in a small chapel located in a cancer hospital called La Divina Providencia, Archbishop Romero was assassinated with a single bullet to the heart.[56] A few days before his murder, he had declared, "If they kill me, I shall rise again in the Salvadoran people. I am not boasting; I say it with the greatest humility."[57] Jon Sobrino writes, "With Archbishop Romero, God has visited El Salvador."[58]

Living the message of Christ is not an easy journey to undertake; it is certainly a challenge and can even become a cross. Following the life of Jesus as Church is not just preaching the Word, saying Mass, or administering

54. Ibid., 19–20.
55. Ibid., 21.
56. Wikipedia, "Óscar Romero."
57. Sobrino, *Witnesses to the Kingdom*, 41.
58. Ibid., 53.

the sacraments, but rather the active participation in the mission of the Incarnate One who was sent by God to the poor of Israel and to the world. It is encompassing the gospel life and making it one's own, and wherever it leads, "to follow Christ." It is getting one's hands dirty working in the midst of the impoverished in the spirit of Archbishop Oscar Romero, Dorothy Day, and the many who have sacrificed their lives on the altar of life in the service to Christ. The Catholic Church has been enriched by those who have mirrored the saints and been willing to go beyond their own self-serving interest for the mission and message of Christ.

The Example of Reinhold Niebuhr

Those who live the gospel message of Jesus Christ are also openly and actively opposed to those who breed injustice in the workplace for the sake of profits: the rich wealthy aristocrats. For poverty and injustice are not the whole of reality but represent the failure of human beings in the service of others that are at the heart of any challenge to the Church. To Jon Sobrino, in qualitative terms, the poor who suffer injustice are bent down under the weight of existence, and their most important and difficult task is mere survival in a world of the bottom line by those who measure the means of human production as dollars and cents. Sobrino goes on to say that these poor unfortunates are silenced, robbed of dignity and words to speak, for their spirits are sifted like the sand on the beaches of the world for profits. The poor who suffer from injustice are impotent and powerless to declare and claim their human rights; they are disdained by the affluent, for they cannot do what the imposed culture requires of them. The poverty stricken are considered insignificant, counting for nothing, and are increasingly non-persons within the machinery of economic production. They have become indigent because everything in life that is near and dear to them, especially their dignity, has been snatched away.[59]

Living the message against the proponents of injustice and oppression are people like Reinhold Niebuhr, who witnessed injustice and abuse in the sweatshops of the automobile factories in Detroit, Michigan. To Niebuhr, his calling as a minister and teacher would in so many ways resemble a spiritual journey in social justice. He led not in the way of the socialism of the former Soviet Union but with a sense of fairness and justice to the American workers that literally slaved to earn a meager day's wage. Niebuhr's voyage was a

---

59. Ibid., 139.

journey through the unknown passages of life that inspired him to accept the challenge that religion can, and should, promote social change for an improved and equitable life to those suffering from injustice in the workshop. These were the places where lower-level workers were abused, exploited, and dehumanized for the sake of profits—a personal affront against the Creator. Time and again, history is replete with such examples. To Sobrino, "unjust poverty is the deepest wound in our world."[60]

Reinhold Niebuhr began his public ministry in the early 1920s, ministering to a humble church of seventy parishioners in the city of Detroit, Michigan, a town that was mostly controlled by Henry Ford. It was there that Niebuhr encountered widespread injustices that were directed toward the working-class populace because of their efforts to unionize—workers often referred to as the means of production and considered less than human even by the churches. He discovered that blue-collar workers, who were taken advantage of by upper-class management, were also abused by the supervisory staff as well. Following this discovery, Niebuhr became a staunch advocate for unionizing the blue-collar workforce, especially at the Ford Motor Plant, and, quite possibly, any large company that employed lower-level workers. He soon became the spokesman for those who had no *voice* in the workplace. Undoubtedly, Henry Ford and his fortress of cronies detested Niebuhr, for he publicly criticized Ford while backing the labor movement in the automotive industry for the inclusion of higher pay, safer working conditions, and reasonable benefits.[61] Sometime in the mid-1920s, Niebuhr took a tour in one of Ford's automobile factories. The visit was appalling. The men worked under horrific conditions, resignedly sweating through the ungodly heat of the giant sweatboxes. It was unbearable to watch and obviously the scene touched his spirit. It gave Niebuhr the sickening feeling that the face of labor was empty.[62]

My father, the late Peter J. Calvanese, was a labor organizer and business representative for the Philadelphia Brotherhood of Painters, Paperhangers, and Allied Trades for more than thirty years. He never would have tolerated such deplorable working conditions such as those that Niebuhr found in Detroit. Dad believed in and fought for the rights of working men, which included the right to a living wage and safe suitable working conditions. In the early years of his career, Dad was considered a union

60. Ibid., 138.
61. Niebuhr, "Religion Fosters Social Criticism," 246.
62. Ibid., 246.

radical too, probably much the same as Niebuhr. Through ignorance, then, it is understandable why Niebuhr was labeled a "communist" by those in control of the means of production, including many in the churches.[63] That insult led psychologist Wayne Dwyer to argue, "If you label me, you negate me." It is apparent that because of his deep sense of compassion for the lower-level working class who felt the whips of injustice Niebuhr felt negation from the rich wealthy businessmen and church leaders of Detroit. As a Lutheran minister, somewhat paralleling the ideas of his former student, German martyr Dietrich Bonhoeffer, Niebuhr critically questioned his fellow clergymen as to why they focused on just the personal ethical issues of their congregations, while neglecting the real message of Christ, which is that of caring for the poor, the helpless, and those who suffer injustice. After a while, it appeared that he gave up hope on organized religion's ability to promote justice in society—a thought that may cross the minds of thinking Christians today. Shortly after "The Great War," Niebuhr became a strong defender of Marxism, calling his first book, *Does Civilization Need Religion?*[64]—a question that begs an answer even today. He agreed with Marx that the reactionary role that organized religion shared with the world was unequivocally true. For Marx and Niebuhr, it appeared that organized religion had all the trappings of large corporations and none of the benefits for the poor struggling workers.[65] In a corporate structure there is usually a president, vice president, middle management, supervisors, and the line workers, much the same as in the Catholic Church with the pope, cardinals, bishops, and priests, all of whom at times attempt to control the laity with law, condemnation, and authority. These are the pontificators of religiosity, a group of individuals that, now and then, resurrect the negative images of the Pharisees and Romans. For the most part, Niebuhr, like Marx before him, believed that organized religion can often become counter-revolutionary, which often endows repressive governments with the aura of sanctity and justifies suffering as a just punishment for sin. It also dampens unrest by offering rewards in the blissfulness of heaven while turning a deafening ear to the tears and pain of the poor, the oppressed, and those who suffer indignities in the workplace. Niebuhr came to believe that religion protects the status quo by promoting social unfairness and inequality, thus encouraging an unconscionable pharisaic feeling of righteousness in

63. Ibid., 248.
64. Ibid., 245.
65. Ibid., 247.

those that benefit from its control. Undoubtedly, religion serves as the "opiate of the people" and the ideological cover for established authorities.[66]

Niebuhr was convinced that with the support of prophetic understanding of religion, churches could foster the proliferation of social change for the good of all. Accordingly, he developed the theory of "prophetic religion," a premise for him that stimulated the critical and realistic assessment of the dynamics of human existence that cultivated the eager and insightful depiction of humans and the world. He worked to reveal and sustain the ethical standards that had prompted prophetic criticism and social unrest as well as the prophetic spirits that arise in many generations and cultural contexts. Niebuhr teaches that established social, political, and religious positions must break free from the chains of class struggle. He contends that prophetic religion is able to denounce anyone, including kings, clergy, educators, or executives, who betray the rights of ordinary people by resisting the cries of the suffering worker. Lastly, prophetic religion defies the plight of the poor and the abused workers as it is grounded in the critical realism and functions in society as catalysts for social change. Therefore, Niebuhr's theory of prophetic religion seems to be designed for the betterment of all people, and can very well be the most radical force in the secular world to help transform all Christians—not just analyze them.[67] This form of religion, as Niebuhr argues, is crucial for the future of the churches. Prophetic religion, therefore, can be likened to yeast in dough, for which the reform of religion can permeate political and social structures so as to effectuate a transformation for people to live better lives in societies that can be enlightened in the Spirit of Jesus Christ. It can be the most radical force in social life.[68] Theologian Leonardo Boff has likewise concluded that a prophetic notion of social change is mandatory; he argues, "The sin of injustice is a poverty that is produced by social relations of exploitation. It has to do with impoverishment on the one hand and enrichment on the other; it is the generator of true injustice, which is the sin that God despises; it challenges God Himself."[69]

Niebuhr certainly saw injustice, humiliation, and mistreatment of lower-level workers at the automobile plants in Detroit. Clearly, he asked himself, "How could this be? What can I do to help these people live decent

66. Ibid., 242.
67. Ibid., 263.
68. Ibid., 241–65, paraphrased.
69. Boff, *Saint Francis*, 54.

lives?" As a man of God, he realized that the lower-level workers needed a living wage and better working conditions in order to raise their families and live with a reasonable degree of dignity. It probably dawned on him, as it did to Dorothy Day and eventually Archbishop Oscar Romero, "What would Jesus do?" Niebuhr attempted to elicit the support of organized religion, only to find that the churches seemed oriented towards the Fords of the world: the rich, powerful, and wealthy aristocrats. Niebuhr believed that religion had the responsibility to care for the needs of its people through social justice, and the only help and support that he ever received was from the Protestant Bishop Charles David Williams, whose early death left him in a state of near despair. With Williams' transition, Niebuhr was determined to undertake to change the face of religion through a concerted effort for social change, rather than to continue the focus of most church leaders, who focused on personal morality and the perfection of one's soul. Niebuhr felt that if he cared for the physical welfare of the community through social change and attempted to lessen the strain of class stratification, care of one's soul would soon follow.[70] But the struggle for social change in Detroit seemed overwhelming, and eventually he lost hope in the churches doing what was needed for the working poor. In 1928, Niebuhr, obviously in a state of disappointment, left Detroit and took a position as Professor of Social Ethics at Union Theological Seminary in New York City. His aim there and for the rest of his life was to foster social change through the prophetic word and the ministries of his energized students.[71]

The Need for Challenge in the Church

The need for social justice that has been affirmed by Reinhold Niebuhr and liberation theologians is to challenge the Church in its responsibilities to the impoverished as an absolute must in order to cultivate the faithful children of God in the image of Jesus Christ. As Jon Sobrino has concluded, "It is necessary and healthy."[72] Sobrino goes on to say that it is the martyrs who silently challenge the Church's economic, political, and ideological structures, those that stand up and take an active prophetic role in the ultimate elimination of poverty and its related sufferings. This fundamental challenge to the Catholic Church consists in holding leadership account-

70. Niebuhr, "Religion Fosters Social Criticism," 246.

71. Ibid., 265.

72. Sobrino, *Witnesses to the Kingdom*, 134.

able for its past and present actions towards the crucified people of Christ: the poor, the hungry, and the abused children of God. This is the Church's primary responsibility and ultimate challenge. "But," as Sobrino argues, "this questioning goes unheard."[73] Once the martyrs are dead and buried and far from the thoughts of the Church, their challenges seem to have lost their effect. It seems that Church leaders find their comfort zone when the martyrs are silenced and stay dead. Then it is liturgical business as usual. The tragedy in the aftermath is the ever-deepening problems that occur while the Church impoverishes itself by dehumanizing the potential of the martyrs, the souls that have gone before and have contributed so much of their lives to liberating the poor. They should continue to challenge the Church "to bring the people down from the cross of Christ."[74]

Sobrino believes that the Church of today has declined significantly after Vatican II. It still calls itself the *ecclesia Semper reformanda*, as Vatican II has acknowledged, or as the fathers proclaimed in much stronger words: *casta matron*. This much is clear: the Church has made some progress in its ministry of liberation. But compared with the Church of the mid-1960s that emerged from Vatican II and the synod at Medellin, there recently have been undeniable setbacks in its prophetic ministry to those that suffer abuse and hunger. The crisis continues to this very day. Sobrino argues that "the signs of deterioration are unconcealable, for that is the direction that we are now moving."[75] The concerns that haunt the Church of today are not so much the limitations or sins it encounters. It is the lore of moral credibility. Among these related concerns that can be listed are the reoccurring scandals from the past to the present and the Church's failure to adapt and attract new followers. The distress that troubles the contemporary Catholic Church is the loss and decline of the *good* that was once real and meaningful to all those Catholics who placed their hopes and dreams in a better way of being *church*. Often these were the poor that had sought the Church's help, only to encounter the opposition of the rich and powerful members that were tightly associated with the hierarchy. These include the failure to embrace the values that are now dying the death of a thousand bureaucratic details.[76] Sobrino claims that we can still reform the Church of the future. He asks, "where is the audacity of Medellin? Where is the courage of

---

73. Ibid., 135.
74. Ibid., 135.
75. Ibid., 135.
76. Ibid., 139.

a Romero to risk everything to save the poor and abused of this world?"[77] What Sobrino is demanding is that the Church stand up for the poor, the hungry, and those that suffer from injustices. The Church must go out and risk its position and posture in the world of the rich and wealthy. Because the Church is now so positioned in a sort of comfort zone, an equanimity that embellishes the notion of staying the course and not rocking the boat, Church leadership is afraid to offend their rich and powerful friends by taking an active role in alleviating poverty in the world. The Church, in the view of Sobrino, is unfortunately accustomed to considering the poor as those to be addressed only in social-pastoral practices; in other words, the lower-level ministry that is not associated with the hierarchy of the Church. But at the essential levels, as exemplified by Archbishop Romero, where ecclesial identity and the true ecclesial power are at stake, the Church does not always give the impression of being *real* if, in Sobrino's words, "it is not the Church of the poor."[78] For some, the leadership of the Church seems *plastic* as a result of its lack of effective commitment to the poor, the hungry, and those who suffer from injustice. On one hand, too many of its leaders are afraid of conflict and struggle, while on the other, they often do very little to solve the problem of poverty for fear of the ramifications of concrete actions and the Church's standing in the political world.[79]

The hope and dream for Sobrino is that the Church can once again be an attractive light to the world, however, he laments the lack of the most essential key to its credibility as a moral force for all to embrace:

> The Church does not see its being and doing in the context of the poor, but in other contexts-which may be necessary and even good, but are unrelated to the Church's essence. At the moment of truth, such things as institutional organization, the struggle with the sects, maintaining church attendance and an alienating religiosity, obsessive faithfulness to the Magisterium, and a long list of etceteras count for more than the reality of the poor.[80]

This unreality for Sobrino is more than any possible theological exaggeration, which places at risk the deepest identity of truth, justice, and faith in the Church. To view it from another perspective, the Church must revaluate its views on the essentials of *faith, hope, and charity* in the teachings

---

77. Ibid., 135.
78. Ibid., 140.
79. Ibid., 140.
80. Ibid., 141.

of Jesus Christ. Genuine Christian faith must be based on the cross of the suffering Christ and his blessed resurrection. To think otherwise would be a misinterpretation of Christianity and a distortion of the Church's role in the world. Some of the more affluent members of the Church have claimed that times have changed, that the cross is good and necessary in the liturgy, in private devotion and in personal life, but in their way of thinking the cross and resurrection have nothing ultimate and serious to say in the social reality that the Church seeks to evangelize. This is simply not *truth* according to the gospel! Concurrently, there have been some helpful positive changes in the political scenery. But, to Sobrino, it would be a serious mistake to confuse that optimistic view with the true reality of the cross. Changes in the organizational structure, the modification of Mass, or other outer manifestations of Church identity have very little to do with the deeper theological or metaphysical aspects of Catholic Christianity. The values that are most important to the sustenance of Catholicism are love of God, love of neighbor, and the acceptance of the gospel of Jesus Christ. It is serving others less fortunate, those that have nothing to offer the hierarchy of the Catholic Church except devotion to the cross. For by the love of the faithful will the world come to know that people are genuine Christians and citizens of the world, because of their poverty.

It is only as the leadership of the Church views the world through genuine Christian eyes that are not blinded with the human debris of heartless affluence, but is sympathetic toward victims of the worlds iniquitous systems, that they can look back to their origins through the pages of the Gospels with faith in a loving Savior, and look forward to the future with hope. It all begins with Christ's love for the poor, the hungry, and those that suffer injustice. God is not found in the majesty of Vatican City, or the touristy artifacts of Rome, but in the face of God, which is found in our sisters and brothers in need, the poverty stricken children of Jesus Christ. Archbishop Romero once declared that "the Christian who doesn't love the poor is not worthy to be called a Christian."[81]

Karl Rahner has clearly pointed out that the Church's first responsibility is ministry to the poor, the oppressed, and those that struggle for daily existence. He feels that it is not enough for the Church to empathize with the poor at Sunday Mass, but rather, it should do something concretely to rectify a problem that is long overdue for the Church's worldwide ministries. This in itself can constitute an immense challenge for the Church. To Rahner,

---

81. Ibid., 136.

the Church must be the catalyst that brings the rich and powerful face to face with the sorrows of the poor and the abused. It must bend their ear and squeeze their priorities until they see the wisdom of Christ in the face of those enmeshed with suffering. The Church, then, must go out into the world to help the poor and abused. It must gather a veritable army of faithful followers to go forth and to do God's work by joining the ranks of Dorothy Day, Archbishop Oscar Romero, Gustavo Gutiérrez, and many others who have spent their lives assisting and caring for those that have been oppressed far too long: the poor and suffering sisters and brothers of Jesus Christ.

4

Obstacles in the Ecumenical Movement

Hope for the Future, Obstacles to the Present

ECUMENICAL THEOLOGY IN WHICH Catholic Church is now involved originally surfaced in Protestant missionary Christianity following a four-century fallout from the Reformation. What grew from this lengthy break from the Roman Catholic Church yielded a new and different theology, the "search for harmony" that is accompanied by the long-term prospect of unity within a newly pluralistic Church of Christ. This resulted in a dialogue among several diverse denominations that developed from region to region in Western Europe and culminated in different ways of practicing the Christian faith and new interpretations of dogma that, collectively, opened the door to reconciliation of deep divisions that still exist among the various Christian confessions.[1]

Although the bishops at Vatican Council II, in the "Degree on Ecumenism," sought the unification of Christianity, they inserted certain caveats into the documentation that seemed to act as a wedge rather than a more irenic step of rebinding toward that desired unity. Acknowledging that some of the other denominational confessions had presented themselves as true believers of Christ, the bishops noted significant differences in hermeneutics, praxis, and cultural habits, giving the impression that Christ himself was divided. These dissimilarities were, for the majority of the bishops, a stumbling block in the journey toward eventual ecumenical

1. Flannery, ed., *Vatican Council II*, 514.

union.² For the bishops assembled at Vatican II, acceptance of basic principles of Catholic dogma were deemed essential for communion with non-conforming communities. Fundamentally, an accord with separated confessions necessitated acceptance of the teaching that God's grace become the prerequisite for unity. The bishops strongly affirmed the requirement that the separated Christian confessions can only be reunited with the Catholic Church by those who, at a minimum, profess the triune God and the proclamation that Jesus Christ is Lord and Savior of all. Simply stated, ecumenical unification would only be achieved by those who accept and practice the gospel according to the main tenets of standard Catholic doctrine.³ To the bishops at Vatican II, belief in God's love as revealed through the death and resurrection of the Incarnate One is paramount for reconciliation with the separated churches and Rome. For the Catholic bishops, the communal experience can only be accomplished through the profession of faith in Jesus Christ as Lord as the "sacrificial lamb" who offered himself on the altar of the cross. This is the fundamental belief for Catholic Christians that binds the faithful with Christ that is seen in the scriptural prayer of Jesus as mediator with the Father, "that we may be one with Christ who is one with the Father" (John 17:21).⁴ Christ Jesus is, then, in this dogma, affirmed as the primary source of oneness with God. Also, this concurs with what Saint Paul has proclaimed: "There is one body and one Spirit, just as you were called to the one hope, one calling, one Lord, one faith, one baptism" (Eph 4:4–5).⁵ To the bishops, therefore, concern for restoration of unity with the Catholic Church and other confessions requires more than agreement among the clergy alone. What is required from Vatican II is full concordance and participation of the faithful, for which all are obliged to cooperate, whether practicing Catholics, theological scholars, or teachers of religious studies. Christians declaring communion with the Holy Spirit are then called to affirm the "bond of community" that exists in harmony with God's loving will.⁶

The bishops at Vatican II supported this belief that there could be no ecumenism worthy of the name without interior conversion.⁷ With this

2. Ibid., 499.
3. Ibid., 499–500.
4. Ibid., 500.
5. Ibid., 500–501.
6. Ibid., 507.
7. Ibid., 508.

attitude, affirming ecumenical unity through the intercession of the Holy Spirit, the fathers at Vatican II affirmed the supportive notions of self-denial, unstinted love, and true humility. This included service to others, forgiveness of sins, and authentic desire for unity with all Christian sisters and brothers from other denominational confessions. The bishops concurred, in so many words, with the separated confessions that the Church in the past had made mistakes and desired pardon by proclaiming the written word of 1 John 1:10, "If we say we have not sinned . . . his word is not in us." Thus, in humble prayer, the bishops appealed to forgiveness from God and their separated sisters and brothers from other confessions.[8] To the Council at Vatican II, "this change of heart, along with their shared holiness of life with private and public prayer for the unification of Christianity should be regarded as the very soul of the whole ecumenical movement and merits the name, "spiritual ecumenism."[9] The "Degree on Ecumenism" from Vatican II, moreover, seemed to be an epiphany for the Catholic Church. It was certainly a cultural shift, along with a positive attitude of "aggiornamento," initiated by Pope John XXIII, which stated the desire to open the windows of the Apostolic Church to let in the fresh air.[10] But questions were raised by irate conservatives who claimed that the Council at Vatican II went too far with this notion of ecumenical change and adjustment of their relations with the Protestant denominations. From an alternative view, liberals insisted that the Council at Vatican II did not go far enough. As a consequence, the hardline conservatives became a stumbling block in the progress for change and adaptation to the newly recognized realities of inter-church relations in the ecumenical movement.

According to Karl Rahner, there exists a crisis in the ecumenical movement precisely because of questions in ecumenical theology that often become too problematic and even insoluble. Rahner posits that the insurmountable impasse in the ecumenical movement is a result of not achieving a sufficiently deep realization of what ecumenical theology really is, namely, its starting-point and aim.[11] For Rahner, there are two suppositions that are the beginning from which to understand what ecumenical theology really is, that is, the ultimate assumption in which ecumenical theology

---

8. Ibid., 508.
9. Ibid., 509.
10. http://www.religiononline.org.
11. Rahner, "Some Problems in Contemporary Ecumenism," *TI* 14:245.

Obstacles in the Ecumenical Movement

is based, and what will be the concerns in its future form.[12] Rahner claims that the ecumenical discussions among theologians of the various separated confessions that participate in such dialogue often fail to be progressive and their attitudes less than hopeful with regards to the outcome of the discourse. Usually, the basic assumptions of the talks have been centered on doctrine, for which the average unwary Christian theologian has a tendency to fall into the pit of confessional relativism. On the one hand, it seems that theologians have been inclined to bypass the most important doctrinal differences between the confessions. On the other, professional theologians appear to relate the discussions to the classical differences of doctrine that have already been established by tradition, which include scriptural exegesis, the differences between historical and philosophical modes of expression, and various distortions that have become almost insuperable.[13] Nevertheless, Rahner claims that, by far, ecumenical discussions have been at an all-time high. However, he qualifies his position and argues that the crisis and object of the ecumenical movement, which is that of unification of all denominational churches, still seems distant and slight at best. The main difficulties for him are centered in the orthodox Roman Catholic theology, which, on the whole, is still a long way off from having made the dogmas of the Catholic Church really intelligible and acceptable to the average Protestant theologian. He goes on to say that the differences in dogma are found in the most basic interpretations of Protestant Christianity. The leaders of these churches either cannot or will not overcome these hurdles, ostensibly because they regard such a course of action contrary to their commitment to the principles of the Protestant "freedom of belief." At times, the differences are so great between the Protestant confessions and the Roman Catholic Church that virtual unification often appears impossible.[14] For though all the churches speak of unity, state their will to achieve unity, and declare their convictions to work for unity, despite "all ecumenical resolves," Rahner maintains that the real frontiers in the ecumenical movement still remain "stiff and immovable."[15]

To Rahner, it seems that ecumenical theology suffers from a dichotomy between two opposing and yet similar approaches toward unity, a theory that should be merged into one: "controversial theology and ecumenical

12. Ibid., 246.
13. Ibid., 246.
14. Ibid., 246–47.
15. Ibid., 247.

theology," respectively.[16] Controversial theology is the theological treatment of doctrines considered as part of the official proclamation that had been previously put forward by theologians of the confessional churches.[17] In other words, it refers to the doctrine of theology that grew out of the past, dating from the Reformation, and beliefs that shaped the basis of the differences that created the great divide. For this reason controversial theology solidified the separation of the Protestant confessional churches from the centralized ecclesiastical Church of Rome. Rahner claims that the clashing definitions of the churches appear to be cloudy and ambiguous. He prefers a simpler interpretation that could possibly merge with the more important concepts of ecumenical theology, a paradigm that could simplify ecumenical discussions. Alternatively, then, the use of ecumenical theology could serve as an adjunct to greater hope for controversial theology on the grounds that it contains a better understanding of the theories by which to describe one and the same Christian discipleship, and thus, better able to fuse two assumptions into one.[18] Nonetheless, the first task of a theologian in ecumenical discussion, according to Rahner, is the obligation to explain one's own church's theology to the extent of one's own ultimate self-understanding of that theology in all its breadth and depth. The second task of the theologian should include the clear presentation of one's church's doctrinal views with respect to its origins, historical development, current positions, sustaining principles, and prior assumptions, particularly in cases concerning the differing concepts of truth that lie at the basis of its theology. Thirdly, the theologians involved must submit themselves with a wholehearted will for truthfulness and exhibit the duty and the courage to qualify a particular point of doctrine. This is the deontological responsibility of all theologians in the process of genuine ecumenical discussion.[19]

Rahner's proposal to allow the confessional churches to express their own opinions with the centralized Church of Rome could be a vital thrust towards ecumenical unity. It could demand *a leap of faith* in the act of freely opening the door to dialogue on the way to mutual agreement and acceptance of common doctrines in a renewed ecumenical movement. For Rahner, from clear and unbounded presentations that are reinforced by all theologians' of the separated denominations, the doctrinal observations

---

16. Rahner, "On the Theology of the Ecumenical Discussion," *TI* 11:25.
17. Ibid., 26
18. Ibid., 26.
19. Ibid., 25–26.

Obstacles in the Ecumenical Movement

with respect to their origins, historicity, current feelings, background, practices, and assumptions, constitute the way to learn from each other and to open the mind to discovery of their common truths.[20] He argues further that the primary concern for ecumenical theology—yesterday, today, and tomorrow—is for all Christians to love and serve God in and through the one church of Jesus Christ. And above all, and especially in Western ecumenical theology, this entails loving and serving the *Holy* in and through God's incarnate Son. This is more important than all the invocation of exegetical and biblical theologies of the churches as they attempt to pull together.[21] In recognizing the problems of refining the theological differences of the churches, Rahner concedes the difficulty of reaching an ecumenical agreement:

> We have only to consider the radical differences, which in fact exist between the individual Churches, at least in part, in their understanding of what theology can be or should be at all, and to realize that ecumenical theology considered as a discussion between the theologies of different Churches constitutes an immensely difficult problem.[22]

Rahner has pointed out that the theological participants in ecumenical discussions have a challenging responsibility to understand and deliberate the critical assessments in theologies that are considered uppermost between the separated Protestant churches and the Roman Catholic Church. These approaches, which exist between the differing confessions, are a demanding and difficult task to undertake and unravel in an effort to reconcile the theologies that exist with what they can be in the future. He goes on to describe how a genuine ecumenical theology can challenge the participants involved in ecumenical discussions. At times, talks can occasionally break down, and at that point theologians no longer speak with one another or confront one another. Nor can progress be measured by one another, since genuine ecumenical dialogue appears almost something like a contradiction in terms. The saving grace to Rahner, though, in overcoming these situations is to know and remember that "we must mutually recognize one another as Christians, and therefore, we must bend ourselves again and again to the task of speaking with one another, because there is no

---

20. Ibid., 26
21. Ibid., 27.
22. Ibid., 27–28.

other way whatsoever for us to conduct our human lives."[23] In the ecumenical movement, the obstacles and difficulties on the road to unanimity may exist and quite possibly seem to proliferate at times. That which can help overcome the shortfalls of self-pride and mistrust in ecumenical dialogue is centered in the very idea of knowing that the participating theologians are Christian men and women who recognize one another as sisters and brothers in Christ. Therefore, when in theological discussions, partners must conduct themselves as such, and for these very reasons, they must pray and submit themselves to the tasks of achieving ecumenical reunification.

Rahner claims that in the "Decree on Ecumenism" from the documents of Vatican Council II, we frequently read the word "dialogue," which is a prerequisite for meaningful ecumenical discussion.[24] He claims that ecumenical theology should be a theology of "open dialogue" encouraging all to state their theological positions. In this way, genuine ecumenical discourse offers the unrestricted opportunity where theological opinions can be analyzed, comprehended, and debated so that all will benefit from the spirited "interchange of information."[25] He continues to insist that the objective for dialogue in ecumenical discussion is "truth"—clear, unmitigated truth as all theologians who participate in the talks understand it, know it, and believe it. Ecumenical discussions are not settings for gaining individual converts for one's own church, but for achieving the concise understanding and comprehension of truth; for truth is the essence of dialogue on the path to possible unity in the process of ecumenical unification. Hence Rahner concludes that "theology has to do with truth."[26] Ecumenical dialogue is not merely intended to inform but rather to communicate truth. It is truth that makes a claim valid upon all and should be conveyed in such a way that it is strictly identified with the accuracy of mind, heart, and experience of the theologians who take part in the discussions.[27] Rahner seems to support the notion that if two or more theologians are engaged in ecumenical dialogue, they may think as one will about the nature of truth, the character of theoretical reasoning, or the makeup of truth in the context of faith as it has been interpreted. For him, theological dialogue is not only intended to communicate information but also to speak for truth as it

23. Ibid., 28.
24. Ibid., 29.
25. Ibid., 29
26. Ibid., 30.
27. Ibid., 30.

has been understood and believed. Otherwise, dialogue could deteriorate into a "sociological phenomenon" in which mutual information is merely exchanged with regard to attitudes and opinions on either side of the table.[28] He observes that the mutual presuppositions of ecumenical dialogue are such that they may have only a social significance. For how could the opinion of another, even if it is truth to him, be of interest to a third party if it were not from the outset what it claims to be, or become that other person's truth? Such opinions can become problematic, and quite apart from the fact that dialogue, with truth as its essence, can also be a social reality that plays only one part in determining a specific sphere of existence. Secondly, there entails a far more serious concern in ecumenical discourse other than its social reality, because "dialogue presupposes a pluralism of attitudes, convictions, and aims in the partners to the discussions."[29] The discourse may develop into a serious challenge to one's faith or an allied problem for the participants to ecumenical dialogue. Rahner comments on this problem in ecumenical discourse, saying:

> The real problem of pluralism of opinions only arises at a point in which "de facto" particular convictions have in principle and by their very nature lay claim to a universal validity. They must do this unless they are willing to surrender their own nature.[30]

It seems, no doubt, that Rahner recognizes the problems and difficulties in ecumenical dialogue. For deliberations without a clear objective can frequently break down and quickly turn into a social gathering of meaningless talk, or a mere assembly of theologians with little in mind but to sit, chat, and discuss their differences in theology, or whatever seems to be important to the participants at the moment. In other words, ecumenical discussions without a goal in mind can seemingly deteriorate where there is little joining of theologies or any clear purpose to the discussions. Likewise, there is the problem of pluralism of attitudes and the deep-seated apprehension of seeming contradiction in theology that, perhaps, only a few may agree on. Deep-seated pluralistic attitudes can quite possibly be the greatest stumbling block in a meaningful discussion on any level of ecumenical dialogue. This problem too can doom ecumenical discourse and mutual rejection of one another's viewpoints.

28. Ibid., 30.
29. Ibid., 30.
30. Ibid., 31.

Among the axiomatic difficulties in ecumenical discussions that Rahner points out is the question that often becomes difficult and at times seemingly insolvable precisely because there is no clear sufficient realization of what ecumenical theology really *is*. What is its purpose? Or what are its goals? Rahner claims that when theologians who have taken part in ecumenical discussions from the various separated confessions quickly discover the difficulties inherent in such talks, they begin to take a dim view of the outcome.[31] Rahner notes that this result leads to "confessional relativism" and tends too hastily to bypass the doctrinal differences between the divergent confessions. As a practical matter, this form of dogmatic relativism does not help solve the problems at hand. It seems that too many theological assumptions are sometimes taken for granted in formulating doctrinal differences. In numerous cases, through the method of modern exegesis, the differences between philosophical modes of expression and ideas have become nearly impossible to understand fully.[32] This seems to be an obstacle in achieving the goal of agreement on the issues at hand. One theologian from a separated confession may take the view that his interpretation of a particular passage of Scripture is correct, a belief that is based on the historicity of the scriptural passage in question, while another may think otherwise. At times, there seems to be no end to the potential conflicts. Rahner notes that since Vatican II the Roman Catholic Church has been involved in more ecumenical discussions with separated churches than in previous years. This gathering of separated communities has surprisingly led to an interest in one another's theology, which seems to turn in a positive way toward greater exchange of subjects, viewpoints, and methods, etc. But when the discussion comes to the subject of unity, the notion is often met with only slight acceptance. It seems that the separated confessions still regard the subject of unity as a course of action that is contradictory to their own principle of "Protestant freedom of belief."[33] On this point, Rahner suggests:

> The orthodox Roman theology is, on the whole, still a long way from having made the dogmas of this Church readily intelligible to the average Protestant Christian. On the other hand, within the Protestant Churches, differences are to be found as to the most basic

---

31. Rahner, "Some Problems in Contemporary Ecumenism," *TI* 14:246.
32. Ibid., 246
33. Ibid., 247.

interpretation of Christianity, and the leaders of these Churches cannot, or perhaps will not, overcome this state of affairs.[34]

Rahner continues to point out that the dogmatic differences seem to be so far apart that at times that any unification aspired to between the separated churches and the Roman See is nearly impossible. This is the crux of the problem for ecumenical theology.[35] Rahner sees that the inherent difficulties and obstacles in ecumenical dialogue may never come to a workable solution. He takes notice of an obvious problem of simply recognizing the Christianity of the dialogue partners in ecumenical debate:

> When we conduct an ecumenical dialogue, or pursue ecumenical theology with one another despite the fact of our being divided among many Churches, then, the ultimate necessary condition which we presuppose for this is that each of us recognizes the others as Christians.[36]

For Rahner, the ultimate basis of ecumenical theology is not the theories of theologians, but the power of the Holy Spirit that unites. For through deep understanding, each participant acknowledges in the other the interior presence of the Holy One of God, because those who live in faith, hope, and charity are, in fact, one with the Divine. Accordingly, to Rahner, it is of no concern what the interpretation of theology really is, or whether we name, for example, "sanctifying grace, justification grace, or salvation grace," or whether we believe in the doctrine of transubstantiation or not. What is uppermost is the truth that God shares his divinity with humanity through the outpouring of his loving grace, which, to Rahner, transforms Christians from sinners to justified men and women, regardless of how precise the details are that we may interpret this saving event of justification, or how we choose to express it.[37]

> The ultimate basis of ecumenical theology is that unity, apprehended in hope, which consists in a belief in justifying grace, a belief which, even though in its theological formulation and its explicitation in creedal form, is still in process of being arrived at

---

34. Ibid., 246–47.
35. Ibid., 247.
36. Ibid., 248.
37. Ibid., 250.

and is nevertheless already in existence as one and the same belief in both of the parties involved in ecumenical theology.[38]

Thus, the universal faith that lies at the center of one's humanity through the power of God's grace is the same for all. In other words, all legitimate Christian confessions with the Roman Catholic Church have more in common than one would suppose. This is true beyond all reasonable doubt and, therefore, constitutes the concrete foundation for the ultimate condition of ecumenical dialogue and ecumenical theology for the past, the present, and the future.[39] Faith, then, which precedes all theological reflection or theoretical and social objectification, is present in all Christians of good will through God's "graced presence."[40] On this foundation, ecumenical theology can and should arrive at a consensus on the unity of faith at the level of conscious reflection and socio-cooperative living, given that we already possess this oneness at the level of God's justifying grace. This union in the faith of God, through the power of the Holy Spirit, is the motivating force that implies the possibility and the necessity of ecumenical theology.[41]

From a different perspective, Dietrich Bonhoeffer's ecumenical ecclesiology of Protestant theology seems compatible with the Catholic theology of Karl Rahner. For example, Bonhoeffer's christocentric ecumenism insists, "It is now clear that the ecumenical movement has not merely to do with practical cooperation, information, conversation, and study, but rather the task to confess the faith in the *concrete* situation in which we live."[42] Similar to Rahner, Bonhoeffer espouses the need for truth in dialogue, not just discourse, which could lead to thoughtless discussion that may go nowhere; but rather, an open informational exchange with one purpose in mind—that of unity in truth for all through the gospel of Jesus Christ to proclaim. To Bonhoeffer and his call for repentance, there are two ways of viewing the ecumenical movement: first, "as an association of a utilitarian character; and secondly, as an embodiment of the Church of Christ."[43] Although Bonhoeffer is not a utilitarian in the sense of John

---

38. Rahner, "On the Theology of the Ecumenical Discussion," *TI* 11:33.

39. Rahner, "Some Problems in Contemporary Ecumenism," *TI* 14:251.

40. Ibid., 251.

41. Ibid., 251.

42. Visser 't Hooft, "Dietrich Bonhoeffer and the Self-Understanding of the Ecumenical Movement," 200.

43. Ibid., 201.

Stuart Mill, he appears to posit elements of the concept of the greater good for the greater number of people in the ecumenical process. His primary concern for the ecumenical movement is for "the representatives of the churches to live up to their main obligation, which is to be the Church of all while proclaiming the Lordship of Jesus Christ over the world."[44] Bonhoeffer contends, therefore, that "it is one thing to pray for deliverance; it is quite another to act with Christian courage and compassion in order to deliver those who are faithful and suffer from oppression."[45] There are other ways in which Bonhoeffer influenced the concept of ecumenism which is that of its nature and the extended sphere of its tasks.[46] In a 1935 article, he writes, "the unity of the Christian people and the love for Jesus Christ transcends all frontiers."[47] Bonhoeffer recognizes that the right and nature of the ecumenical movement is to provide "fraternal help, warning, and correction" to Christendom. Its task, he claims, is to underscore the notion of fraternity in which he was a staunch believer in the anti-Nazi Confessing Church's claim, "we will never be ashamed of the voice of our brothers."[48] To Bonhoeffer, then, the ecumenical movement should be a "fellowship of churches that are their sister's and brother's keepers, as in a family in which mutual correction is the norm."[49] It seems that Bonhoeffer's deeply felt notion of ecumenism is underscored by the reflection of its ecclesial character. It is not the mere idea that the ecumenical movement is an invitation to an introverted preoccupation with the church, or a community isolated from the world, but rather, a "church for others" that is centered in the notion of servant leadership as emulated by Jesus' washing the feet of his followers (John 13:5–8). For Bonhoeffer, this is the mission of the church of Jesus Christ, which is that of love, service to others, and becoming a beacon of hope in the darkness of night. Bonhoeffer claims that "an ecumenical movement which is simply another United Nations, with a religious varnish, cannot help the world."[50] The ecumenical movement must bear witness to the authority of *truth* and *unity* of all the churches. It must openly oppose those that would espouse the practice of violence, racism,

---

44. Ibid., 201. Dr. J. J. Oldham echoed Bonhoeffer's statements.
45. Kelly and Nelson, *Cost of Moral Leadership*, 38.
46. Visser 't Hooft, "Dietrich Bonhoeffer," 202.
47. Ibid., 202.
48. Ibid., 202.
49. Ibid., 202.
50. Ibid., 203.

and social exploitation of the weak. Bonhoeffer insists that the ecumenical movement of the world's Christian churches "must ask itself at every stage of its life, whether or not, it is on the way toward that goal."[51]

Ecumenical Theology of the Future: Toward Church Credibility as a Moral Force for Good

The question for the present is this: what will ecumenical theology be like in the future? According to Karl Rahner, ecumenical theology in the foreseeable future will not place an emphasis on "unification" between the separated communities and that of the Roman Catholic Church; it will not remain the same as in the present or that which has been pursued in the past.[52] Rather, ecumenical theology of the future will in all probability be separate and distinct. For as churches and theologies grow and change throughout the years, so will their ecumenical concepts be modified and become transformed. However, as Rahner has claimed, "this premise cannot be taken in a sense, which implies that the ecumenical theology of today and that of tomorrow no longer have very much in common."[53] Moreover, ecumenical theology may change with the times, but the very basic common substance of Christianity will never change: the crucifixion and resurrection of Jesus Christ as the core belief affirmed in what Rahner calls the "hierarchy of truths."[54] However, it seems that he supports the notion that "the borderline marking the transitions between the present and future are of course fluid, and it follows that the same also applies to the ecumenical theology of today and tomorrow."[55] Rahner insists that the ecumenical theologian of the future "must always proceed from two starting points: not only the notion of ecumenism, but also the official zeal of faith from the Church";[56] theologians must think outside the confines of ultraconservatism, while expanding new, creative, and innovative questions. Rahner claims that the ecumenical theologians of the future must extend fresh concepts while seeking new possibilities that may bring the separated churches closer in truth with the ecclesiastical Church of Rome without

51. Ibid., 203.
52. Rahner, "Ecumenical Theology in the Future," *TI* 14:254.
53. Ibid., 254.
54. Ibid., 254.
55. Ibid., 255.
56. Ibid., 255.

the necessity of overt public unification. In other words, theologians of the future must seek out the common ground of faith in Christianity without surrendering to the tensions that sometimes result from the pressures of achieving public unification. This can only be accomplished through a passionate interchange of dialogue that is faithful to the official convictions from his church. Therefore, Rahner concludes:

> The situation in ecumenical theology has changed precisely as the general situation of the churches and their theologies has changed. Formerly the churches and their theologies had only each other as partners and their opponents in the discussions, at least so far as Europe was concerned. Today, it is different.[57]

Presently, it seems that the Catholic Church is beginning to lose its influence in the world. Its acceptance appears to have significantly lost its luster, especially in Western Europe. Although it still officiates, at times, in public and official events, the Catholic Church and its theologies, individually and collectively, find themselves in a *diaspora*. And without any firm ground in which to stake its claim as a moral leader, the majority of Christians in Europe, and perhaps America too, have divested themselves of any overriding hierarchical influence on their morality. It seems that many of the faithful, so far as their philosophy of life is concerned, cannot be described as Catholic in any real sense other than being culturally Catholic in name only.[58] Therefore, according to Rahner, before the Catholicism of the future is reduced to a "historic relic" in the shadow of its past, the leadership of the Church must seize the opportunity to develop new perspectives towards this present age as it really exists. For this is the cultural age of the greater mass of people, of increasing unification of political spheres in human history in a world that was formerly segmented into rationalism, enlightenment, and pluralism controlled by the technology of the mass media, of modernization, and whatever terms along these lines one may choose to characterize still further this era.[59] For Rahner, then, "Theology consists in a conscious reflection upon the message of the gospel in a quite specific situation in terms of the history of the human spirit in coming to terms with a quite specific *Zeitgeist*, or spirit of the times."[60] Hence, if the soul of theology is the gospel in relation to the human spirit, which must

57. Ibid., 255.
58. Ibid., 255.
59. Ibid., 256.
60. Ibid., 256.

be viewed from different perspectives depending on the state of one's specific history and era, it follows, then, that the ecumenical future of theology depends on a continual application of the gospel in relation to the human condition of any new age in keeping with the churches' foundation in the message of Jesus Christ.

The Ecumenical Movement Today: The Church's Hope for a More Credible and Attractive Future

The first official symposium of the more official ecumenical movement took place in Amsterdam, Netherlands, in August 1948. It was a gathering of Protestant, Eastern Orthodox, and Russian Orthodox theologians who attempted to set a goal for *unity* within the Christian framework that had, for too long, been fragmented. What emerged from the discussions was the birth of the World Council of Churches (WCC), an organization of separate confessions that assembled for the dual purpose of developing solutions to the moral and social problems that beleaguered all peoples, and to create the unification of a divided Christendom that seemed deluged with pluralistic thinking, theological differences, and individual ritualistic practices.[61]

In 1950, at the World Council of Churches first Central Committee meeting in Toronto, Canada, the group clarified its relationship to all of the member churches with the following declaration: "the World Council of Churches is not and must not aspire to become a super-church; its purpose is not to negotiate unanimity between individual churches but to bring all confessions into living contact with one another and to study the issues of church unity for the good of all. The World Council of Churches cannot and will not base its perspectives on the conception of one church alone; and it does not, by necessity, accept a specific doctrine concerning the nature of church unity."[62] The committee, then, proclaimed that the World Council of Churches is an organization of Christian denominations that accepts the Lord Jesus Christ as Savior and Son of God, and thus functions in unison to carry on the work of its two world movements: "Faith and Order," which objectifies its concern with matters of faith and seeks out the discovery of agreements and appreciation, in dialogue, of the differences among each of the various confessions; and "Life and Work," which is a goal concerned with the practical side of Christianity and the cooperation between all

61. Kallos, "Historical Sketch of the Ecumenical Movement."
62. Ibid.

churches in the application of Christian principles that are foundational to the ethical and social problems of the modern era. Hence, the World Council of Churches, through "Faith and Order" and "Life and Work," facilitates the common good of Christianity by promoting and sustaining the growth of ecumenical consciousness in the members of all its churches.[63]

Although the Vatican did not formally recognize the World Council of Churches in its infancy or support its efforts in the ecumenical movement, there was no official cooperation until the late Pope John XXIII invited the World Council of Churches representatives to participate as observers at Vatican Council II in 1963. This positive gesture from the pope opened the window of opportunity for the Roman Catholic Church to become involved in the World Council of Churches and participate as an observer in the future efforts of the ecumenical movement in the quest for unity with all Christianity. As a result of this opening from John XXIII, his successor, Pope Paul VI, journeyed in 1964 to Jerusalem to exchange the "Kiss of Peace" with the late Ecumenical Patriarch Athenagoras I. This historic milestone finally linked the gap between the Roman Catholic Church and Greek Orthodoxy for the first time in some five hundred years. Subsequently, on December 7, 1965, the most dramatic and momentous act of ecumenism took place, concurrently, by Pope Paul VI at St. Peter's Basilica in Rome and by the Ecumenical Patriarch Athenagoras I at St. George Patriarchal Cathedral in Constantinople: "By joint statement, both leaders nullified the excommunication of 1054 CE. And by mutual consent, the 'anathemas' were consigned to oblivion."[64] This was the first major step for the Catholic Church in the process of achieving unity in the ecumenical movement.

According to Cardinal Walter Kasper, former president of the Pontifical Council for Promoting Christian Unity, "The ecumenical developments of the 20th century were welcomed in the Catholic Church long before the Second Vatican Council officially took part in the movement."[65] Kasper claims that in the first half of the century many theologians, including Paul Couturier, Yves Congar, Jan Willebrands, Hans Urs von Balthasar, Karl Adam, and many others, followed in the footsteps of Johann Adam Mohler and John Henry Newman, who had prepared the way for the Church's attitude toward the ecumenical discussion that pointed the way to unification. The premise, they noted, was founded by Christ himself on the eve of his

63. Ibid.
64. Ibid.
65. Kasper, "Ecumenical Movement in the 21st Century."

crucifixion: "That all may be one" (John 17:21).[66] Even the late Pope John Paul II called the decision to strive for unity in the ecumenical movement "irrevocable and irreversible." This ambition became one of the primary objectives of his pontificate. His successor, Pope Benedict XVI, immediately after his election, reaffirmed the same commitment in the following words: "Following in the footsteps of my predecessors, in particular Paul VI and John Paul II, I feel intensely the need to affirm again the irreversible commitment assumed by the Second Vatican Council and continued over the last years. Thanks also to action of the Pontifical Council for Promoting Christian Unity."[67]

Today, the current status of the ecumenical movement has not been without its challenges, difficulties, and misunderstandings and seems to be in a state of transition. Nonetheless, strides toward the reality of unification seem to have been positive. The Catholic Church, for its part, recognizes the great work of the members of the World Council of Churches and their sincere attempt to unify all churches. The Church's relationship with the other confessions no longer considers them as enemies or competitors, but rather as sisters and brothers in the spirit of Christ on the common pilgrimage towards full communion. Regardless of this newfound relationship, the Catholic Church does not overlook the vast differences in theologies; for example, the dissimilarities in political and institutional critique of the ecumenical movement, which originates from the fundamentalist groups as well as some of the older more venerable churches and their theologians too. It seems to some of the other confessions "that ecumenism has become a negative term, something that is equivalent to syncretism, doctrinal relativism, or indifferentism."[68] To Kasper, the World Council of Churches in the twenty-first century seems to have in mind the changing conditions that will certainly influence any renewal of the ecumenical prospective. On a global level, he states that "we observe on the one side unions and alliances, a huge number of bilateral and multilateral ecumenical consensus, or convergence of documents; on the other side, there seems to exist tensions and even new divisions often due to questions of ethics."[69] He notes also the questions that result in the context of emerging new communities of an evangelical and Pentecostal character, confessions who seem not interested

66. Ibid.
67. Ibid., Quoted from *L'Osservatore Romano* (English ed.), n. 18, May 4, 2005, p. 3.
68. Ibid.
69. Ibid.

in ecumenism, if not openly opposed to the ecumenical movement itself.[70] The Catholic Church cannot mandate conformity. This transitional period of the ecumenical movement must evolve by itself into its full potential and not be hampered by the efforts of the few. The partnership presently enjoyed by the Catholic Church and other confessions must continue to heal the scars that were left from the dark ages.

Looking forward into the future, it has become the Church's position to solidify the respective positions of all Christian churches, by focusing on efforts of the ecumenical agreement, such as "common Bible study, exchange of spiritual experiences, gathering of liturgical texts, joint worship in services of the *Word*, better understanding of our common tradition as well as our existing differences, co-operation in theology, missionary work in cultural and social witness, co-operation in areas of development, and environmental conservation, and in segments of the mass media, etc."[71] For the Roman Catholic Church, spiritual ecumenism and a renewed ecumenical formation of the faithful are important in this transitional period in history. At the same time, Kasper points out that the ecumenical movement of the twenty-first century should develop a new vision, a goal that is foundational to the spirit of unity and the commitment of those who participate in ecumenism by finding a path on the journey towards a common future. As part of Kasper's new vision for the future of the ecumenical movement, he has developed a five-point program that, in his opinion, is what the Catholic Church's position should be in regards to its participation going forward into the twenty-first century:

First, the ecumenical movement must be clear in its theological perspectives. This he sees as an absolute necessity for the unilateral understanding of the participating churches. Clarity is essential. With such clarity, theologians can grasp the meaning and purpose of the ecumenical discussions with a greater degree of certainty. The basis of the ecumenical movement from the outset should be centered on lucidity of purpose—not like the house that was built on sandy soil, where when the winds blew and the storm came it fell to the ground (Matt 7:26).

Secondly, all theological discussions should be Christ-centered, as this understanding forms the constitutional basis of the World Council of Churches and underlies the essence of Vatican Council II. For Christians are united through the communion of faith in one God, one Savior, Jesus

70. Ibid.
71. Ibid.

Christ, and the one Spirit who unites all through the commonality of baptism. For baptism makes possible the individual confessions to give each other the true meaning of being genuinely Christian, even though we have not yet achieved full communion.[72] Thus, the continuation of the dialogue on baptism and the mutual recognition of our unity are essential to the future of ecumenical relations. The World Council of Churches should reinstate the use of the document on "Faith and Order," the text that confesses one faith. "For without this inclusion, ecumenism may become vague and ambiguous. Therefore, the Catholic Church asks the World Council of Churches to reinstate this important inclusion and give it the momentum it originally had, both in the ecumenical movement and the program of the World Council of Churches."[73]

Additionally, Kasper emphasizes the question: "What do we understand by visible unity of one faith and one Eucharistic fellowship expressed in worship and the common life in Christ through witness and service to the *Word*, as the Constitution of the World Council of Churches states?"[74] Without an answer to this question the ecumenical movement would surely fail, "for without a vision the people perish."[75] The Catholic Church's understanding of unity, as full communion in faith, sacraments, and ministry, is compatible with the acceptance of its Orthodox and Oriental Orthodox sister churches; but unfortunately, it differs from the most usual interpretation of mainline Protestant positions, especially the Lutheran denominations. The Catholic understanding of "unity" is not to be mistaken for "uniformity." For the Catholic Church, "unity that is understood as communion implies, unity in diversity and diversity in unity. But, in the same way, as unity should not be confounded with uniformity, so plurality should *not* be identified with contradictory doctrinal pluralism or indifferentism about our respective confessional positions."[76] Hence, indifference can never be a solid basis on which to build ecumenical relationships. Ecumenical discourse presupposes partners that have their own clear identity, and only then can they appreciate one another and their different identities by entering into meaningful and fruitful dialogue. For dialogue that presupposes truth can be more than just an exchange of information; in

72. Ibid.
73. Ibid.
74. Ibid.
75. Ibid.
76. Ibid.

Obstacles in the Ecumenical Movement

some ways, though, theological discourse is an exchange of gifts that each of the respective churches can share; it is relative information in theological discourse where all can learn from each other. Therefore, ecumenism in the twenty-first century must be coherent in the faith, honest in its purpose, and truthful in its orientation and goals; it should be something where partners can have a shared vision with a common theological ground on the meaning of church and unity.[77]

From the third perspective, Kasper claims that "there is no ecumenism without conversion; and there is no *future* at all without conversion."[78] He points out that renewal and conversion of hearts include both "personal" and "institutional" aspects. On the one hand, personal conversion and renewal entails the change of attitude towards one another's virtues, which leads to the purification of memories from the experiences of the bitter past and the avoidance of unfair polemical statements, thus preparing the way for reconciliation. This personal conversion and sanctification implies a spirituality of communion, which for the Catholic Church, means "to make room for the other and to withstand the egoistic temptations of competition, careerism, distrust, and jealously."[79]

On the other hand, he claims that "institutional reform is an essential presupposition and condition for ecumenical progress."[80] It is here that Pope John Paul II refers to the Church as marked by "the 'structures of sin; for it is at once holy and always in need of purifying reform. The Church, therefore, should follow the path of penance and renewal."[81] It is now time for the Church to gather new spiritual forces for a new epoch into the future. But there can be no doubt, as the ecumenical partners and many of their own faithful have reminded the churches, that unity is far from the end of the road. The ecumenical movement needs renewal and reform, and the same revitalization that is required of all its partners, if it is to make a difference in this new century.[82]

From the fourth viewpoint, Kasper claims that the heart and soul of the ecumenical movement is "spiritual ecumenism," a concept that is neither vague, weak, sentimental, irrational, nor subjective, but a phrase

77. Ibid.
78. Ibid.
79. Ibid.
80. Ibid.
81. Ibid.
82. Ibid.

that means none other than that Spirit of Jesus Christ to those who confess "Jesus is Lord" (1 Cor 12:3). This is its true meaning, that of the teaching of Scripture, the living tradition of the Church, and the outcomes of ecumenical dialogues that have been personally and totally assimilated and filled with the life of Christ—"the way, the truth, and the life" (John 14:6). Thus, "Mere ecumenical activism becomes an empty soulless bureaucracy destined to exhaust itself."[83] Theological academia, on any level, that does not include the heart and soul and spirit of Christ, are simply words that are lifeless with very little or no meaning. Spiritual ecumenism that begins and ends with a prayerful spirituality in communion with faith in Jesus Christ contains all the elements that are necessary for the presence of Christ to be affirmed. The late Pope John Paul II reminds us that another important form of spiritual ecumenism is found in the martyrs of the many churches, Orthodox, Catholic, and Protestant; hence, "the blood of the martyrs contain the seeds for new Christians."[84] This is the blood that was spilled for the sake of Christ, which informs the spiritual unity that may one day bring the churches together as one.

From the final point, Kasper focuses on the notion of "practical ecumenism." In practical ecumenism, unity with the Catholic Church is not a goal in itself, but rather an instrument or sign of hope. From the objectives of the Catholic Church, unity is the anticipation of the churches' communion with all of Christianity, if not all with humanity.[85] Therefore, "the universal context of the commitment for the unification of the churches has further implications for social and political *diakonia*, practical witness, and for the dignity of the human person and for human rights, for the sanctity of life, for family values, education, justice, peace, health care, the preservation of creation and last but not least, interreligious dialogue."[86] In all of these fields the churches can work together, for within the spirit of cooperation there can be developed closer relationships. But as experience has taught in the past, these practical problems can also have a negative impact on the relations of the churches, something churches cannot afford to have. The ecumenical slogan "Doctrine divides, practice unites" is, therefore, all but *a priori*. Kasper argues this same startling point: "Already in the past, political implications were often responsible when theological conflicts ended with

---

83. Ibid.
84. Ibid.
85. Ibid.
86. Ibid.

divisions within the churches, and today secular political options have often a similar effect."[87] What is required today and into the future for the healthy development of the ecumenical movement is *sober, self-critical theological reflection* and *discernment of the Spirit*.

The Catholic Church sees and rejoices in the progress that was made in the ecumenical pilgrimage in former centuries. Presently, the Church must center its goals in light of a new beginning and clarify its foundation, its vision, and the ways of its role in the ecumenical movement. Above all, the Church must be centered in the christocentric belief of spiritual ecumenism. [88]

Conclusion

In sum, Cardinal Kasper's five points seem to contain valuable insights and guides for ecumenism in the Roman Catholic Church's relations with the World Council of Churches. Although the Church is not an official member of the World Council of Churches, it is a full member of the Faith and Order Commission and serves on the committee for Mission and Unity in a consultative nature. The Church also sponsors faculty appointments and spiritual support at the Bossey Ecumenical Institute, Geneva, the international center for encounter, dialogue, and the formation of the World Council of Churches. Through the Pontifical Council for Promoting Interreligious Dialogue, the Church works with the World Council of Churches team on interreligious dialogue and cooperation. Even though the Catholic Church is not as yet a certified member of the World Council of Churches, it does continue to participate in the discussions with the Joint Working Group, those who co-sponsor yearly meetings in order to discuss issues of common interest and to promote spirit of cooperation in socio-political issues. The Joint Working Group is a worldwide group of individual confessions that consists of seventeen members and consultants who represent the World Council of Churches constituency of church traditions, confessions, regions, and religious professionals, such as the ministries of ordained women and men. An equal number of persons are nominated by the Pontifical Council for Promoting Christian Unity (PCPCU). Both groups discuss issues of the day that affect their interrelationships, and they share experiences of their individual churches and constituencies with the

87. Ibid.
88. Ibid.

Roman Catholic parishes on the local level.[89] This cooperation has been praised by Reverend Dr. Olav Fykse Tveit, General Secretary of the World Council of Churches. In his words, "I don't want to comment on the membership of the Roman Catholic Church in the World Council of Churches at this point, but it is important to say that there are many ways for us to work together and some of them we already have in place; and they can be strengthened and we can find new ways also."[90]

Although the Catholic Church involves itself in many of the programs of the World Council of Churches and participates in various commissions and subcommittees, something seems to be missing. Both sides of the table talk of unity, the convergence of theologies, the relevance of sacraments, and the conversion of hearts, but what does it mean if those aspects of the ecumenical discussions have not been agreed upon or disseminated among the laity? Are the talks just for the sake of theologians and the hierarchy? What good is such information, however important, if it is not shared with the faithful? People in the Church, i.e., the laity and the priests in the field of ministry to their parishes, have a God-given right to know what is going on in the center and the higher levels of Church governance. If it is unity that the hierarchy desires, and it certainly seems to be so, then it needs to be shouted from the rooftops, so the world knows what the churches are about. If the Church desires to be true to its "Decree on Ecumenism," then it must join the World Council of Churches and, weekly and monthly, work to achieve its ecumenical goals with an open mind—not just passively, but actively. Today, people in both the secular and religious world seem to be hungry for something more tangible than what is offered by traditional religious practices. The laity seems to have lost a sense of the gospel of Jesus and his prayer for reconciliation and unity, and what it means to those who now live aimlessly in the darkness of disunity. As Noam Chomsky has claimed, "The problem with most people is that they don't know that they don't know." Many people today live in the utter bliss of ignorance. Christ is there for the "taking." All the Church has to do is to reach out and touch the hearts of people, not with authority and pontification, but with Christ-like love, understanding, forgiveness, and compassion to all. The time has come for the Catholic Church to become proactive by updating its hierarchical thinking for Christian unity and become conversant with the practices in the contemporary world. The Church could thus eliminate the rigidity of

---

89. World Council of Churches, "JWG with the Roman Catholic Church."

90. Mackay, "Church Unity Remains Top Priority for WCC."

its past absolutism and promote its growth in a future of hope in peaceful communion with all the segments of the Christian churches. The Church must reverse its present downward trend toward isolation by seeking out new ways of returning to its origins in Jesus Christ and of growing the fold for saving souls for God through Christ. In this venture toward ecumenical unity, one finds the brightest hope for restoring Church credibility and attractiveness in a world come of modern age.

In the following chapter, we will look at the possibilities for the Church in the future from the various perspectives of creative theologians like Timothy Radcliffe, Karl Rahner, Johann Baptist Metz, and others who see the face of a Church that is changing, not by its own hand, but by the intervention of Holy Spirit, in those who love the gospel and aspire to love and serve God in the renewal of the Church's original commitment to the life and teachings of Jesus Christ in communion with God's Holy Spirit of Love.

5

The Possible and the Necessary in the Future Church

THE QUESTION TO BE considered by the Catholic Church in the present age remains: what are the possibilities in the future if the Church remains rigid and inflexible toward change and modernization that is necessary to be a relevant example of Christ in the world? Is it possible, if the Church does not address its antiquated practices, relatively soon, that it may inevitably erode from within to a mere fraction of the worldwide influence it once enjoyed? Although no one can accurately predict what will happen in the future, one thing is for sure: adhering to the same old rules and policies will only produce much of the same old results. Ignoring the necessary changes that are now facing the contemporary Church is rather obvious to all of Catholic Christianity. Now is the time for *renewal and reform* and to seize the moment before the Church's apparent decline becomes, seemingly, irreversible.

It has been said that the only thing that is permanent is change. Although this cliché does not apply to the truths of Scripture, it certainly is applicable to many of the practices, rituals, and canons of the Catholic Church. For these were often created by humans at some point in time to serve a meaningful purpose in that temporal context. Now, however, by all appearances, it is time for some of those structures, once thought to be absolute, to be changed and modified through adaptation to a different era. Reasonable modifications are in order to stem the downward trend of *relevance* for so many Catholic believers today. It is time for leadership to take

The Possible and the Necessary in the Future Church

a more proactive role in its renewal process and once again to reinstitute Pope John XXIII's call for the *fresh air* of pre-Vatican II's "agiornamento."

Following the conclusions of Vatican II, the Church should exhibit greater openness to change and more consistently practice the concept of *ecclesia semper reformanda* while it struggles to keep up with the times in an ever-changing world. For it is very possible that if the leaders of the Church do not implement the call to adapt its thinking and practices to a new generation of parishioners, change may happen in spite of it. Church leadership has been cautioned, as were the first followers of Jesus Christ, to "read the signs of the times" (Matt 16:3).

Theologian and former Superior General of the Dominican Order, Timothy Radcliffe, proposes that "the shape of a tree is the fruit of its interaction with its environment. Its leaves receive sunlight, which converts it into sugar; the roots burrow deep into the soil for nourishment and water; and the bark is its vital skin. The tree exists in itself, of course, but it is only alive in multiple interactions with what it is not."[1] For Radcliffe, the shape of the church to come will also be determined by how it interacts with its world, and how it faces the dilemmas that have shaped religions of the world, including *Judaism since its beginning*. Radcliffe's ultimate recommendation is to avoid assimilation into a secularized society that could lead the Church to a "ghetto-like mentality" and its ultimate disappearance, which becomes, in essence, another form of death. In order to grow into the future through the peace of Christ, it seems that the Catholic Church must adjust to present-day society by adapting to changing times, while staying focused as the community of Jesus' followers that it was from its inception. The Church should free itself from enchainment from its more rigid past, and emerge from its outdated structured history in order to come forward into a new world with fresh new ways of being church in its thinking and acting. The Church may thus offer the world the dawn of a new *spring* by entering into the new age with a renewed spirit of evangelization that would help the Church appeal to a younger generation of followers, while still retaining its relevance for the faithful of all ages.[2]

As far back as 1864, Pope Pius IX, in his "Syllabus of Errors," condemned as an error that the pope "can and should reconcile himself with progress, liberalism, and recent updates in civilization." So the Church was seen, then, as necessarily opposed to democracy, freedom, new ideas, and

---

1. Radcliffe, "Shape of the Church to Come," 21.
2. Ibid. 22.

science. But time and again, the Church was seen as out of touch with reality in such matters. Now that we are at the threshold of a new century, it is time for the Church to begin the process of reinventing itself, by returning to the roots from which it came and grew like a mighty tree, espousing attitudes of simplicity, forgiveness, compassion, and love to all, while practicing the gospel of Jesus Christ.[3] According to Radcliffe, in his program for the revitalization of the Church, Jesus was a man of conversation, someone who lived the simple life, a savior who forgave sinners and shared love and compassion with those who were downtrodden, poor, and abused. If Jesus did not exercise his authority and power in an overbearing way, should not the leadership of Church do the same? This approach would certainly contrast with the culture of control and oppression of authority the hierarchy have practiced in times past and present. Is there any logical reason why the Church cannot be an oasis of Christ's freedom while proclaiming the notion of an *open church*, a church where people are not intimidated by the centralization of power or threats of a heavy handed reprisal? People who have been divorced and remarried, gay or lesbian, or those who live in some other irregular way may, for example, wonder whether they could still belong to the Church or whether they could ever be considered anything more than inferior Christians. Where can such people find Christ's unconditional love, forgiveness, understanding, and compassion in today's Church? One may ask, too, what of priests who have left their ministry and married and are now raising families in the spirit of the Lord? Could they return to their ministerial roles in the Church? What of women who have been ordained to the priesthood? Could they fulfill a mission in the eyes of the hierarchical Church? Are these people to be regarded as outcasts? Radcliffe suggests, "If the Church is too have a healthy and complex interaction with society neither retreating into the ghetto, nor going down to the plughole of assimilation, then, we need a dynamic Catholic culture."[4] To achieve such a "dynamic Catholic culture" would, at the same time, demand that the faculties of universities and colleges have the freedom and confidence to explore the Christian faith, by asking difficult questions through investigation of possibilities of future theological directions without the threat of intimidation or exclusion from mainstream Church activities, or the suspension of their teaching license.[5]

3. Ibid. 22.
4. Ibid. 23.
5. Ibid. 23.

If this mighty force of creativity, which was once the center of Church credibility, is to flourish and grow far into the future, it is necessary to maintain a moral vision that neither locks itself in a ghetto-like mentality nor assimilates itself into a totally secularized society. The Church is neither a sect that is hermetically sealed from the world nor a group of people who happen to share a number of non-controversial opinions. The Church is not like a bridge club that meets on Sundays. Rather, the Church should be filled with clergy who aspire to the notion of *servant leadership* in order to maintain the loving vision that engages all Christians as *the people of God* in the twenty-first century, a Church that follows the *Word* of Christ Jesus with compassion, love, understanding, and forgiveness.[6]

A Community of Sisters and Brothers

From an additional perspective and like-minded concern for the Church, theologian Karl Rahner offers an alternate concept of what he expects to find in the future Church. He believes that, although it is possible that the Church may significantly diminish and perhaps disappear in its present form, the only certainty that will be left behind and continue into the future will be the gospel *Word* of the Lord that will proceed on its course through the ages. He affirms, too, with Jesus Christ, that even the gates of hell cannot not prevail over the community of those who believe in Jesus Christ as their Lord and Savior (Matt 16:18–19). One of the most important beliefs for the Christian of the future is the anticipation of that which is hoped for and prayed for. Rahner's aim is not to exalt the Church as an end in itself, but for the Church to be faithful to its calling to represent the "kingdom of God," a kingdom that lives within those who proclaim that Jesus Christ is their Lord and Savior.[7] He goes on to point out the possibility of there coming into being four individual scenarios for the Church of the future:

First, Christians of the future cannot expect a homogeneous Church that is similar to that of medieval times. It is possible, he concedes, that the Church of the future can only exist as the "Church of free believers, those who think and believe outside the confines of a totalitarian state and far from the fears of condemnation, intimidation, excommunication, or being silenced. In this view, the Church must be the champion of all: believers and non-believers alike, gathering the harvest of those who are lost and living, albeit

6. Ibid. 23.
7. Rahner, "Perspectives for the Future of the Church," *TI* 12:202.

in a state of darkness and isolation from secular society."[8] The Church of the future must return to that of its origins and become, once again, the Church of Jesus Christ's followers at the level of social living and community. It must have the missionary will at its roots and the attractive zest for the gospel that is to be preached to all peoples, so that all in the world can embrace Jesus the Christ in baptism with the hope for the future that can be imprinted upon the *social orders* of contemporary times. In this, the name of Jesus Christ will be recognized by the leaders of the world, and Christianity will be not merely an affair of the private conscience of the few, but comprised of those who are part of society and among all peoples of the planet.[9]

Secondly, the Christian community of the future would have a quite different sociological structure from that which it now enjoys, both in the mainstream churches and in the various groupings that claim to be Christian. It is possible that the communities of the future, whether at the level of a local church, a diocese, or the Church in the universal sense, will be composed of like-minded individual churches and communities. These future churches will differ from one another only in respect to their juridical constitution, to the point where differences of opinion involved could be encouraged and lead to a pluralistic union of the churches bonded principally in their commitment to Jesus Christ. Viewed from this prospective, these future communities would exist through the gospel in faith, hope, and altruistic love. It is conceivable that, in the future, this renewal would encompass the majority of Christians in the world, in a manner not unlike a United Nations under Jesus Christ. Such a Church of genuine sisterhood and brotherhood will exist to the extent that people can unite themselves within the community of Christ Jesus, in the spirit of mutual love and service to the *least* of peoples. And it will be such love that can motivate and assist official Church leaders of the older ensconced in ecclesiastical structures to adapt themselves to the contemporary world. The only authority in the community of such a future Church will be the power that is derived from the mission and message of the gospel. And the only official position that will exist will come from Christ to those who are mandated to lead—not in a sociologically prestigious capacity, or with all the influence and the benefits that often go with authority, but rather from the attitude of humble service. Christians of this Church would experience free faith, a willingness to share their lives, and the sisterly and brotherly love of all people within a genuine worldwide Christian community.

8. Ibid., 202
9. Ibid., 203.

The Possible and the Necessary in the Future Church

In this future, every believer would rejoice with gratitude to God when God's grace makes it possible for individuals to take the burden of official leadership in the Church upon themselves, a task that brings no earthly honor and no worldly advantage, but only the self-effacing satisfaction of being chosen to become, as Jesus Christ has exemplified, *the servant to all* (Mark 9:35).[10] In this regard, Rahner claims that the individual church communities of the future will have to create their own social unity for themselves, and to a certain extent, a renewed church will be the outcome and reward of their own planning. These church communities must not seek to be self-sufficient in human terms or seek to provide everything that a human being needs in the way of human fulfillment—culture, security, spiritual comfort, and neighborliness. The community of the future must be open to the outside world and be ready to be shaped by individuals who obviously and wholeheartedly engage themselves in the moral, spiritual life of the pluralistic societies of their secular world. They will share in its struggles, in the self-commitment that such service requires, and in the pluralism of movements, to better their societies for their common good. Hence, the church communities of the future will exist in the spirit of sisterhood and brotherhood that engages the interests of the secular world with agape love, compassion, and neighborliness.[11]

Rahner goes on to say that the future pastors of these churches will be those who have a theological understanding of Scripture, intelligence, understanding of their culture, and experience in serving others. They would be endowed with a charismatic and religious personality aided by an experiential knowledge of the world they also serve. He recognizes that in future generations the lack of priests will become so severe that the strenuous demand for pastors in church communities of the future might be led by none other than a presbyter or elder. He also notes that the Catholic Church of the future may ultimately develop a more modern and practical understanding of celibacy. And this, in turn, could be coupled with rising of the *diaconate* level of ministry or those in the order of the married *permanent diaconate* to the priesthood. This would help make up for the critical lack of priests.[12]

Third, the Church of the future would find new ways of making the Creed and gospel more meaningful and attractive to the faithful. However ancient the gospel may be, the meaning, freshness, and relevance continues

---

10. Ibid. 207.
11. Ibid., 208.
12. Ibid., 209–10.

today and into the future, as it was at its foundation two thousand years ago. The gospel would be translated and preached in such a way as to give the faithful renewed hope, greater strength of faith, and the spiritual guidance that is filled with love in order to overcome the challenges and obstacles of the present-day secularized world. For the many, life can be so difficult and burdensome that they need the inspirational message of Jesus Christ as the source of all inspiration. Individual followers must never hear that they are threatened with fear and condemnation for their failings. What they need to know is that "God is love and forgiving" (1 John 4:8). People need to know that Jesus is there for all to embrace through the spirit of the gospel, for the gospel of Christ can strengthen those burdened with difficulties, challenges, and obstacles, In other words, the leadership of the Church, present and future, must find contemporary meaning in the message of the written *Word*, and to correlate the gospel to the community with spiritual direction for the day, allowing its message to spring up ever afresh through a meaningful outreach at gatherings, Sunday worship, or in people's everyday existence.[13]

Fourth, Rahner claims that the most "ecumenical theology" of all is the theology that in practice speaks to the credible concerns of the people of today and tomorrow. The theologies of the separated churches would achieve their most fruitful encounter and complete understanding if each, from their point of departure and historical background, transforms themselves through a theology of the future church that is based on a mutually recognized "hierarchy of truths." For then, all Christian churches in a pluralistic world would everywhere and in all countries of the world have the status of a diaspora church. And all of the churches, including the Roman Catholic Church, would have to reckon in the future with a greater degree of pluralism among the theologies, spiritualities, and moral principles that are upheld within each of the separate churches.[14] In the civilized world that has become one and homogeneous, the different religions by necessity can no longer exist in the long run without the mutual influence and "interpenetration" of one another. Rahner goes on to note that the spirit of cooperation must become paramount. He adds: "this exchange of Christianity will be the determining factor, because even from the empirical point of view it is the most comprehensive religion, the one that allows for most variations, and is least of all attached to a specific cultural milieu."[15]

13. Ibid., 210–11.
14. Ibid., 214–15.
15. Ibid., 217.

To Rahner, therefore, the future does not simply arrive in the course of a natural unfolding or as a blind fate. Instead, it is wrought out in the solitary decisions of the heart. In the final analysis, then, the Church's task is not to orientate itself to a future already worked out beforehand; rather, it is necessary to create one's mission in a spirit of unreserved commitment and hope, fashioning it by one's own choices and decisions. This is so because, in the end, there is only one message: if the Church believes and commits itself to hope against all hope, as the Apostle says and Abraham did, then this commitment of faith with total and unreserved dedication which it involves, will of itself usher in the future, which God has promised to his church and to those who believe in Jesus Christ.[16]

Call for a Second Reformation

Johann Baptist Metz, noted for his writings on the subject of political theology, asserts that the birth of the Reformation was not just a subject of remembrance but an object of hope in the future of Christianity, an occasion that brought about a positive change for all Christendom. As an activist Catholic priest, Metz claims that this means the Church must integrate the question of change into its structures and adaptability as well as an awareness of the circumstances that inspired the Reformation into a more Christ-centered relationship within the era of Martin Luther, including the present age and far into the future for Christianity in a post-bourgeois society.[17] The Reformation was situated within the disappearance of the medieval-feudal world and the emergence of the so-called *bourgeois world* of the Renaissance. The Catholic Church, also, had to cope with the later resultant birth of the Industrial Revolution, which recognized the possibilities for expansion of its influence, and thus quickly associated itself with this newfound wealth. Ultimately, then, the bourgeoisie came to be regarded as the *real Christians* in the sense that they financially supported the Catholic Church and exerted their influence and political clout, which, naturally, the bourgeois controlled.[18] To Metz, "if we use the terms, bourgeois and the bourgeoisie in a purely historical way, we are now situated at the historical end and turning-point of this bourgeois world."[19] For him the

16. Ibid., 217.
17. Metz, *Emergent Church*, 48.
18. Ibid., 48.
19. Ibid., 48–49.

Church presently stands within the disappearance of this bourgeois world and the pending dawn of a post-bourgeois era. This would be a time when Christianity would be able to preserve and develop its historical identity with its roots, when, as a totality, it achieves a "second Reformation." The Catholic Church, then, "must succeed in eating, as it were, a second time from the tree of Reformation knowledge."[20] Unfortunately, because of the immobility that the present world's political blocks have created, there has emerged a false sense of stability and confusion, which could lead to a further contagious disturbance of the Church's credibility and relevance. More accurately described, the Church exists at this point where one age is closing while another is opening. In this there exists the possibility for the radical change that can break through once again, but in a new way with important implications for the future of the Catholic Church. How can God's salvific grace be experienced?[21]

The connection between the grace of reformational freedom and the Church's mission to be a credible moral force in the various societies in which the Church is active has always been central to its absolute concern for the future. Metz argues that the human person of today is part of this late-bourgeois world. This world encompasses people who are stretched in their church life between doubt and commitment, between apathy and a superficial kind of love, between ruthless self-assertion and weak forms of solidarity with the Church. Such people often seem confused and more uncertain of themselves and their identity with the Church than ever before in history.[22] But for today, the puzzlement for churchgoers is whether and how the Church mediates grace and provides meaning in the everyday lives of its people. One might ask: how would such a second reformation take place within the Church's possibilities for revolutionary change to make it more relevant and attractive in the post-bourgeois world? Metz interprets such a new reformation in its literal sense as a *restoration* of the Church's original relationship and connection through Jesus Christ. This must take place before one can speak of a second reformation as a grace returning in the spirit of freedom to its original calling in Jesus Christ, and as a special grace enabling the Church to offer moral leadership to the political world.[23] It is obvious there has developed over the centuries a historically power-

20. Ibid., 49.
21. Ibid., 49.
22. Ibid., 49.
23. Ibid., 50.

ful bourgeois Christianity marked by a dualism between the ecclesiastical world and the world of bourgeois materialism. There seems to have been developed among the bourgeoisie at the same time an understanding of human happiness strictly oriented to property, competition, and success, with material prosperity overarching the whole. In other words, the Church has become oriented to the notion of materialism that utilizes the biblical texts as a so-called divine foundation for possible goals of monetary gain.[24] This is a condition that all Christian Churches must avoid.

To Metz, Roman Catholicism must hold firmly to the insight that one cannot remove the grace of freedom without obscuring or even destroying the effectiveness of the Church to promote the spiritual life and a genuine Christian embrace of peace and justice against war and injustice in the contemporary world. Freedom appears, in fact, to be insufficiently imbued with the freedom of God's children in a peaceful life in their secularized world. Metz claims that God's gift of freedom parallels that of the Protestant Reformation, born in the freedom to dissent from Roman authoritarianism. This freedom offers a new way of being church in which the teachings of Jesus Christ takes on new life for the Christian churches in which the grace of freedom, the Spirit of Jesus Christ, and the gospel teachings were conjoined.[25] The Roman Catholic Church claims to be a mediator of grace to political governments, an assertion that includes an affirmation of the Holy Spirit's gift of freedom to speak in peace to a militarized world. As such, freedom is a central dimension of the courage to follow Christ in their way of being church in the truth by which their life in Christ is directed, and in that life the church can become a "light unto to the world," showing the path to peace and justice in the modern age (Matt 5:17–20). Catholicism obviously has a very broken relationship to the bourgeois notion of freedom in modern times. The so-called "Catholic Age" within this historical process was always—at least within the Middle European cultural era—a stage for acting and being controlling in the history of Church domination prior to Vatican Council II. The Protestant model of grace of freedom is being spread out in the history of the Reformation up to the present day and involves freedom of the individual person who, in the presence of his or her loving God, is no one's unthinking slave or obedient servant; the freedom of the Christian person has led to a complex interplay between church and state in a mutual quest for peace and justice that Jesus Christ taught and exemplified

---

24. Ibid., 53–54.
25. Ibid., 56.

to his followers.²⁶ Given this development, Metz concludes that this model of the Christian church attains the freedom to change and to adopt the grace of freedom to affect genuine Christian moral values in the political policies of even a secularized society. In a future ecumenical Christianity, this may include the Catholic ecclesial model in which the individual believer experiences himself or herself not in isolation, but in solidarity with a faith-filled community, free to think and choose his or her church life in the presence of God, for such *freedom is a gift to all of God's children*. In this process, it is the faithful people who become free, who experience themselves as called forth and liberated to become subjects of their own history in the presence of God. According to Metz, therefore, the reformational invocation of grace as freedom and the invocation of grace in a theology of liberation from injustice and war must represent Catholicism today, for the reformational hour of freedom has indeed come to the Catholic Church.²⁷

The analysis of grace through the Church involves, therefore, the grace of being a vortex of peace and justice to the nations of the world. In the grace of freedom, which he attributes to the Reformation's spirit and the grace that can return greater freedom for Roman Catholicism, there emerges a spiritual energy in the political life of the nations where the Christian churches can exert their influence. Metz conceives that the survival of humanity itself is at stake in world politics. This is an evident need for the Church to offset the stagnation of politics as usual in today's society bereft of the moral values that the Church teaches on issues affecting life's challenges and problems of militarism and injustice. In other words, the Catholic Church must be involved in the everyday life of people outside any constricting religiosity or doctrinal declaration that is unrelated to the real world, where people live and work in their everyday being.²⁸. It seems the major social, economic, and ecological questions can be resolved today, but only through the fundamental changes among people in communion with their churches. The issue today, for Metz—and this applies in a special way to politics—is that the churches should learn to *live differently* and to embrace a wide-ranging political theology in order that ordinary people should be able to live their lives in peace and justice.²⁹ Living differently, to Metz, should indeed become a characteristic mark of Christians who

26. Ibid., 57–58.
27. Ibid., 58.
28. Ibid., 60.
29. Ibid., 61.

dare to follow Jesus Christ and who truly believe in his free and liberating presence, and in his intimate connection to the human experience. Metz argues that the mission of the Church involves offering constraints in governmental policies, not just living under the limitations of the diverse issues of the day unrelated to the Church's life and ministry, but under the abiding presence of Jesus Christ, enabling the Church to be a force for peace and justice that exemplifies moral values in today's world. This cannot be achieved through ecclesiastical boasting or for the Church to continue to operate as in the past. Thus, the grace of being church for the people entails the capacity in their political life to exercise moral persuasion and to see reality with the eyes of society's victims. The Lord himself expressed and exemplified such compassion for the victims of an oppressive society.[30] The Church must follow Christ's example.

The question for renewal in the life of the Catholic Church emerges here in the midst of today's political life. To Metz, the grace of *reformation freedom* could extricate the Church from constraints of continuing to live as a triumphant domineering power and grace, which ultimately makes possible a life in solidarity with people facing ordinary problems of the day. The Church must no longer be dependent upon structures lacking credibility and relevance in today's world. For him, the grace of reformational freedom passionately resists any form of solidarity that can be reduced to structures of absolute control by mass conformity and fear. This grace unconditionally demands that the Church enforce its own social identity with Jesus Christ, not in opposition to weaker groups and classes deprived of socio-economic power, but rather in solidarity and communion with the poor and downtrodden, with whom Jesus himself identified. In other words, Christians should live in communion with one another, all faiths, races, and even separate political ideologies in a pluralistic world. This is the grace of *reformation freedom* that should enable the Church to stand as the exemplar of gospel values and to inspire moral sensitivity in a secularized world.[31]

To Metz, this *second Reformation* will not come from the creative thinking on the part of the Roman Catholic Church, or from other denominations found in Western European Christianities, but rather, the second Reformation will come about from the liberation of Christianity by the churches living among the poor of the world, from the people themselves, and from those in the clergy that courageously desire meaningful change

30. Ibid., 61.
31. Ibid., 61.

and adaptation in a pluralistic world — those that experience sufferings and struggles to become liberated from authoritative and controlling measures. From the experience of the grace of freedom in these poor churches, the reformational impulse could come upon other churches as well, including the affluent churches.[32] This new Reformation from below can bring about a divinely inspired process that Metz claims will come to be known as the "grass-roots Reformation."[33] This is not something that will burst into the world, as in a charismatic event, such as Vatican Council II, but in a calmer quieter way, unobtrusive in a protracted process from within the Catholic Church. It would become tenacious when accompanied by numerous setbacks and deep-seated antagonisms until it surfaces with renewed strength like the sun on a new day.[34]

According to Metz, this condition exists more abundantly in the poorer areas of the world: places situated in Third World countries in towns and villages that have been labeled "small Christian communities." This form of church life among the poor is where the grassroots level of the Church and society have bound together their Christ-like values that are expressed in religious and societal lives. It is here that the people assimilate into their Eucharistic *table fellowship*, surrounded by fundamental social conflicts and sufferings. Christians are thus led by the Holy Spirit of Jesus Christ to critically confront those domineering societies that are ruled by powerful, controlling, and repressive bureaucracies. Catholics can, then, become increasingly the freed subjects of their own religious-political history that is imbued with the grace of freedom, conferring on them a renewed consciousness of their emancipation to become more genuine followers of Christ Jesus.[35]

Nevertheless, that the Church as it exists today will never arrive at this process of a second Reformation until the faithful themselves begin finally to take on more diversified forms of genuine Christian praxis at the grassroots level, that is, when they develop in their own situations the basic communities in Jesus Christ, united in the Lord's Supper, and in ministries of service to those in need. Such basic Christian communities would also become the embryonic cells of a new ecumenism, in a more lasting Christian renewal of the churches themselves.[36] And then, finally, the theory of

32. Ibid., 61–62.
33. Ibid., 62.
34. Ibid., 62–63.
35. Ibid., 63.
36. Ibid., 64

a second Reformation in God's gift of freedom can only come from the masses of the Catholic Church, where the laity and clergy together work the fields of Christ, to grow the Church in the spirit of God's loving grace of freedom. *These are the least of those* who will be the faithful to reject the homogeneous bureaucratic mechanisms that have been the demeaning factors of Church policy for hundreds of years.

Presently, the Catholic Church, to Metz, is now at the threshold of a *second Reformation*, an event that will recreate and reinvigorate new possibilities to strengthen the Church to become, once again, a credible, relevant, and attractive force in the future of its Christ-centered ministry. There is always hope in the salvation that comes from the *Spirit of Truth* from the Lord Jesus Christ.

6
Concluding Remarks

Is it possible that Kelly, Rahner, Radcliffe, Schillebeeckx, Gutiérrez Metz, and many other theologians are mistaken in their assessment of the Catholic Church of the present and that of the potential future? In light of the progressive work from the bishops at Vatican Council II, is it still necessary for the Church to change and update areas of doctrines as well as its canonical rules and practices? From all the various perspectives that have been discussed here, it would seem reasonable to conclude that reform is essential in order to reverse the declining trend the Catholic Church has been suffering in so many areas over the past fifty years or so. Many Church practices have even prevented it from moving forward as an attractive and morally credible force in the twenty-first century. According to Karl Rahner, the great machinery of the Roman Catholic Church contains a multiplicity of bureaucratic offices, which Rome reserves to enforce absolute command over its people through its canon rules, doctrinal decrees, and moral laws that cover the smallest details of its control over the faithful. Given this, the frequency of Rome's reactions to particular questions that arise in all parts of the world are certainly not identical with divine law. Therefore, because of the human element in Church governance, these human-made laws are subject to critical questioning and revision whenever the need arises due to difficult circumstances and problems of ecclesiastical and secular history demand new reactions and answers.[1] With these new demands and hu-

---

1. Rahner, "Structural Change," *TI* 20:122.

Concluding Remarks

man needs, it is very possible to eliminate or modify a number of laws and practices of leadership. Otherwise, the continued adherence of antiquated policies could only lead to further erosion of Church credibility and weaken its influence and attractiveness even among its own faithful.

We have examined a few of the issues that have led the Church as we know it into an unfortunate posture of stagnation and a weakening of its moral credibility in today's world. This seems to have occurred as the result of Rome's unwillingness to update many of those obsolete laws that have threatened the Church with decline and ineffectiveness as a visible representation of Jesus Christ's continual presence as *Church*. As we have noted, among the most serious issues confronting the Church of today, and into the foreseeable future, is the lack of priests to minister to the faithful in the parishes. Vocations into the priesthood have experienced a serious ongoing decline ever since Vatican II. Young men today, it seems, lack the desire or willingness to serve the Church in the priestly ministry. This decline has occurred for a number of reasons. The biggest concern of all in this crisis is the inability of Church leadership to permit priests to marry and enjoy the spiritual and psychological benefits of family life. Marriage for the clergy could also be seen as a vocational gift of God's Holy Spirit for the new age dawning in the Church. It is time for the leadership to reconsider the discipline of *clerical celibacy*. Celibacy would then become the option for those who aspire to the priestly life as a special gift of God. It is well documented that even St. Paul recommended that the celibacy he praised should be a choice, rather than a decree or rule to those that follow Christ in the priestly ministry: "A man is better off having no relation's with a woman. But to avoid 'immorality,' every man should have his own wife and every woman her own husband. The husband should fulfill his conjugal obligations toward his wife, the wife hers towards her husband" (1Cor 7:1–3). Likewise, in Genesis 2:18 God himself declares, "It is not good for man to be alone." As one can see in the effective ministries of other Christian denominations, even married men and women can serve the Lord and care for the faithful in their Christian priestly ministry. If in other denominational confessions, including our Orthodox brothers, priest can marry, the Church of Rome in this present era could easily reverse itself and declare celibacy a valid choice for priests rather than a disciplinary rule.

Another possibility that could help alleviate the problem of the shortage of priests is for the Church to reopen its doors with love, reconciliation, and understanding to the nearly twenty thousand men who have left the celibate priesthood and married. This may be the means whereby the Church could lighten some of its concern over the shortage of priests in the parishes. Such a step may take a little careful planning and courageous implementation with the spirit of compassion for the parishioners now bereft of ordained priests. Then, with the stroke of the pen, the Church could include a new assembly of priests in the field—perhaps not twenty thousand, but certainly a significant number of married priests that would be welcomed back into the ministry to help fill the parishes that are in crisis mode and teetering on the brink of closing. For most of the Catholic laity, it makes perfect sense to utilize the assistance of these men by bring them back into the priestly service of Christ.

This leads to the next allied point of womenpriests. The canonical rejection of this possibility arouses in many women the feeling that the priesthood is really an "old boys' club" where women are just not allowed, regardless of personal qualities. However, in spite hierarchy's determined resistance to prevent women from entering the service of the Lord in the priestly ministry, women have already been ordained to the priesthood by a movement of defiant bishops who have disagreed with Rome's all-male opposition. This organization of Catholic "womenpriests" has been on the increase in the United States and Western Europe. Their growth is steadily rising in the face of opposition from the Roman Curia. Without question, the inclusion of women into the priesthood could be an untapped source of spiritual service in the priestly ministry of the Church. The question then becomes: should the Church sanction the ordination of women to fill the gap in the declining number of priests? That this can be accomplished seems obvious given the need and the nature of how hierarchical decision making unfolds in Church governance. If the hierarchy can judiciously interpret the wishes of Jesus in their own favor under the spurious claim that Christ had appointed men only to the original Twelve and thus secured an all-male clergy—even though this may have been the culturally accepted notion at the time—then why not welcome the women who have been validly and presently ordained and are fulfilling the need for a priestly ministry by following Christ in the Church? Jesus himself says, "Do not stop them, whoever is not against us is for us" (Mark 9:39–40). The negative actions of the hierarchy in this instance seem ironic. Even in Church history, Benedict VIII (1012–24) sent a letter to the bishop of Porto, in which one finds that the late pope not only recognized the office of "deaconess,"

Concluding Remarks

but acknowledged that the rite of initiation is an ordination.[2] If that is so, then why not ordain women into the priestly ministry of Christ?

As has been argued in an earlier analysis of the problems with the lack of priests for the Church's parish ministry, there seem no logical reasons why competent women cannot serve in the ministry of Christ as priests if they so desire and believe themselves called to that ministry. It is quite possible that there may be times when a female might do just as well as, if not better than, a male in the priestly service to the faithful. Opening the door to new possibilities for the Church by utilizing the service of women as priests may, in fact, enhance the Church's presence and growth in the contemporary world where everyone has been declared equal, even though the culture at the time of Jesus was dominated by men. Is it not possible and commonsensical, considering the crisis in the Church today, that Jesus himself would agree with the inclusion of womenpriests as a breath of fresh air and a welcomed step for the Church of the future?

There were times in the history of the world when women were regarded as possessions of men, as second-class citizens not permitted to be involved in politics, or speak in a church or synagogue, let alone rule a nation. However, over the centuries this too has changed and women have contributed in many valuable ways toward the betterment of humanity in both secular and religious life. It is now time for the Church to transform itself into a more Christ-like community of believers for its own survival. It must become, at the same time, a credible and exemplary presence of Christ in a world where human needs proliferate, and where Christians continue to depend on their Church for spiritual comfort and inspiration in their ability to overcome suffering from injustice and oppression. Additionally, the declining number of priests has unquestionably had a bearing in the closing of parishes by the hierarchy. Most educated people know that there are shifts and expansions in the demographics of populations, especially in the inner cities. But these socio-economic realities only represent a small portion of parish closings. It seems that the underlying principal of closing a parish lies at the heart of rapidly decreasing number of priests. It seems time for Church leadership to make the necessary changes in their thinking on priestly ministries by the inclusion of married men and women priests. Money and the self-sacrifices of the laity are not able to cure the ills of the Catholic Church alone; the Church should be proactive in mandating structural changes that could restore its credibility and attractiveness in

---

2. Ludlow, review of *Ordained Women in the Early Church*, 133.

its future mission to represent Jesus Christ as "the way, truth and life" (John 14:6), for all the faithful to follow.

In sum, all rules that are set to be followed in canon law must be re-evaluated and updated for the good of all Catholic Christians. This updating involves not merely changing a few elements of the Catholic Mass, or introducing the Latin that was once mandated by the Council of Trent in a more ancient era, but genuine reform in all areas of policy, canonical law, and rituals that can return the Church back to the future of Christianity as established by Jesus Christ and his gospel.

According to the inspiring ecumenical theology of Dietrich Bonhoeffer, Christianity in its very origins was a religion for the weak, the abused, and the oppressed. Prior to his martyrdom, Bonhoeffer stressed that "Christianity stands or falls with its revolutionary protest against violence, arbitrariness, and pride of power and with its plea for the weak."[3] For Christianity to experience a rebirth of its ministry and influence, now and into the future, it must return to its origins and re-proclaim the teaching of Jesus to the young and old alike. The Church should change its previous attitude of authoritarian control, and, as Bonhoeffer has urged in the period of control by Nazi ideology, assume the character of servant leadership in the manner of Christ's life and example. Moreover, the Church should put into practice the way of a Christ-like existence, with compassion, forgiveness, understanding, hope, and love to all sinners—just as it has always been, *a community of sinners*. It is only by returning to its origins in Jesus Christ can the Church determine what it is and where it is going in order to determining its future in a world where people continue to hope for deliverance from suffering at the hands of heartless societies.

There is no question that the fundamental core beliefs of Catholic Christianity, which are foundational in Scripture, will never change. The creedal truths are timeless and constitute the foundation of Catholicism. However, the changes that are referred to in this analysis are the practices and canons that have outlived their usefulness in today's modern world, which form new challenges for Church credibility and influence, politically, economically, and above all, spiritually. "The Church," for Karl Rahner, "is not merely a spiritual community in an abstract sense, but a community of those who believe in the gospel teachings of Jesus Christ, and the example of Jesus telling his followers how to be a community of his saving presence

---

3. Kelly and Nelson, *Cost of Moral Leadership*, 219.

Concluding Remarks

for all succeeding ages. This is a church that lives in communion and love of Jesus Christ—for there is nothing else."[4]

The era of absolute control and authority for the Catholic Church's hierarchy is quickly coming to an end. What is needed for the present and future, as Rahner has concluded, is an "open Church" where all can share in the freedom of God's gift of the Eucharistic Christ to his people. The Church has been called, moreover, to equate itself as the Church of all: saints and sinners alike. Catholic Christianity exists wherever there is faith and love in the forgiving message of Jesus Christ, which offers the faithful none other than God himself. The Roman Catholic Church should be the beacon of hope and salvation through the gospel Jesus for the hopeless, and the source of all truth to those who are searching for something far greater than that which is offered by the societal world. Most people, including lukewarm or cultural Catholics, still need the message of Christ in their lives. They are, too often, fearful of seeking Christ in the Church because they are *not* attracted to it in its stoic practices. These may even be people who are products of the Catholic diocesan school system, or those that at times feel disdain in their hearts for the harsh treatment they may have previously received in Catholic schools. They hunger and search, nonetheless, for spiritual renewal that can still be possible in a revivified parish life that has been neglected to a large degree in today's postmodern society. The Church of today certainly needs reform and renewal to become more attractive, relevant, and a more credible force for justice, peace, and the elimination of poverty in today's modern world. The Roman Catholic Church must reinvent itself by returning to the practices of its origins.

The arguments for recognizing the need for change in the Catholic Church have been reinforced by a recent survey conducted by Beliefnet. com. It found that a majority of Catholics in the United States want meaningful change in the Church. It is interesting to note from their findings that more than 11,400 Catholics responded to some of the most controversial issues of the day, from allowing married men to be ordained, to providing the laity with greater power in the decision-making process of the Church, thus demanding that the Church be more open to Catholics who were divorced and remarried. It is important to note that for all the Catholics who participated in the survey, the greatest concern for American Catholics was *not* the abortion issue, as the hierarchy would lead all to believe, but social justice and the elimination of poverty. Half of the Catholic respondents

---

4. Rahner, *Foundations of Christian Faith*, 326.

said they wanted the Church to become more progressive, while only 28 percent said the Church is "fine as it is." The balance favored return to a more traditional Catholicism. The other highlights from the survey include the following percentages, now reinforced by the analysis of the opening chapters of this study. They are as follows:

- 63 percent of Catholics would like the ban on artificial birth control lifted.
- 56 percent of Catholics would advocate priests being able to marry.
- 87 percent of Catholics would like the Church to increase its efforts in fighting poverty.
- 67 percent of Catholics favored more lay participation in the Church.
- 63 percent of Catholics would like remarried Catholics to be able to receive Communion without obtaining an annulment.
- 41 percent of Catholics think the Church should ordain women.
- 30.5 percent of Catholics believe that the greatest failure of the late Pope John Paul II papacy was the handling of the sexual abuse scandal.
- 58 percent of *non*-Catholics think the Church should allow the use of birth control.
- 86 percent of *non*-Catholics think the Church should reach out more to other faiths.
- 58 percent of *non*-Catholics feel that the Church should ordain women as priests.[5]

Given these statistics, the winds of change obviously exist in the hearts and minds of Catholics as well as Christians from other denominations. It seems reasonable, therefore, for the leaders of the Church to return to the spirit of its origins in simple humility. The hierarchy should recognize in their governance the existence of concern by the faithful parishioners for the problems and difficulties that are presently disturbing them.

In conclusion, the Catholic Church must become the *Church for others*: the poor, the weak, and the victims of oppression, those who are on the edge of faith, and those who question their own Church affiliation too. Without question or retribution, the Roman Catholic Church must return to its roots in order to survive as a credible moral force and grow in its

---

5. Belief.net, "Future of the Catholic Church: Survey Highlights."

Concluding Remarks

attractiveness in the future. Then, once again, the Church would become the community of Jesus Christ, continuing to serve Christ's sisters and brothers, including the outcasts, the poor, and the victims of oppression in a materialistic and violent world. Those who hunger and thirst for peace and justice in the midst of the many oppressive societies in the modern world are the ones to whom the Church is called to represent Jesus Christ in faith-filled service to those in need.

Bibliography

General

Associated Press. "Pope Didn't Know Bishop Had Denied Holocaust: Vatican." CBC News, February 4, 2009, online: http://www.cbc.ca/news/world/pope-didn-t-know-bishop-had-denied-holocaust-vatican-1.845385.
———. "Pope Urges Latin American Bishops to Stem Church's Decline." CBC News, May 13, 2007, online: http://www.cbc.ca/news/world/pope-urges-latin-american-bishops-to-stem-church-s-decline-1.669073. 2009.
BBC News. "Sex Claims Bankrupt US Archdiocese." July 7, 2004, online: http://newsvote.bbc.co.uk/2/hi/americas/3872083.stm. 2009.
Belief.net. "The Future of the Catholic Church: Survey Highlights." April 2005, online: http://www.beliefnet.com/Faiths/Catholic/2005/04/The-Future-Of-The-Catholic-Church-Survey-Highlights.aspx.
Belluck, Pam, with Frank Bruni. "Scandals in the Church: The Overview; Law, Citing Abuse Scandal, Quits as Boston Archbishop and Asks for Forgiveness." *New York Times*, December 14, 2002, online: http://www.nytimes.com/2002/12/14/us/scandals-church-overview-law-citing-abuse-scandal-quits-boston-archbishop-asks.html. 2009.
Boff, Leonardo. *Saint Francis: A Model for Human Liberation*. Translated by John W. Diercksmeier. New York: Crossroad, 1982.
Bonhoeffer, Dietrich. *Letters and Papers from Prison*. New York: Macmillan, 1971.
Brown, Robert McAfee. *Gustavo Gutierrez: An Introduction to Liberation Theology*. Maryknoll, NY: Orbis, 1990.
Brown, Robert McAfee. *Theology in a New Key*. Philadelphia: Westminster, 1975.
CARA (Center for Applied Research in the Apostolate). "Frequently Requested Catholic Church Statistics." Online: http://cara.georgetown.edu/CARAServices/requestedchurchstats.html.
CDF (Congregation for the Doctrine of the Faith). *Declaration on the Question of the Admission of Women to the Ministerial Priesthood (Inter Insigniores)*. October

Bibliography

15, 1976. Online: http://www.vatican.va/roman_curia/congregations/cfaith/documents/rc_con_cfaith_doc_19761015_inter-insigniores_en.html.

Corso, Vincent M. "Facts about Married Catholic Priests." Online: http://www.fathervince.com/mpfacts.htm. 2009.

CPPCD (Conference for Pastoral Planning and Council Development) and NFPC (National Federation of Priests' Councils). *Multiple Parish Pastoring in the Catholic Church of the United States*. Report from the Multiple Parish Pastoring Symposium, University of St. Mary on the Lake, Mundelein, Illinois, February 7–9, 2006. Online: http://emergingmodels.org/wp-content/uploads/2012/05/MPP-Symposium-Report.pdf.

Day, Dorothy. *The Long Loneliness*. New York: Harper, 1952.

———. *Loaves and Fishes*. Maryknoll, NY: Orbis, 1963.

Dulles, Avery. *Models of the Church*. New York: Doubleday, 1974.

"Europe, the Collapse of the Catholic Church." Online: http://newsgroups.derkeiler.com/Archive/Soc/soc.culture.vietnamese/2008-06/msg00878.html.

Flannery, Austin, editor. *Vatican Council II: The Basic Sixteen Documents: Constitutions, Decrees, Declarations*. Northport, NY: Costello, 1996.

Gutiérrez, Gustavo. *Essential Writings*. Edited by James B. Nickoloff. Maryknoll, NY: Orbis, 1996.

———. We *Drink from Our Own Wells*. Maryknoll, NY: Orbis, 1984.

Gutiérrez, Luis T. "Perspectives on Canon 1024." BASIC, October 28, 1996, online: http://www.iol.ie/~duacon/l961004.htm. 2009.

Higgins, Gregory C. *Twelve Theological Dilemmas*. Mahwah, NJ: Paulist, 1960.

James, Larry. "The Wisdom of Gustavo Gutierrez." *Everyday Citizen*, June 15, 2009, online: http://www.everydaycitizen.com/2009/06/the_wisdom_of_gustavo_gutierre.html. 2009

Kallos, John. "A Historical Sketch of the Ecumenical Movement." Orthodox Research Institute, online: http://www.orthodoxresearchinstitute.org/articles/ecumenical/john_thermon_history_ecumenism.htm. 2009

Kandra, Greg. "Camden Announces Largest Closing of Parishes in the Country." Online: http://www.beliefnet.com/columnists/deaconsbench/2008/04/camden-announces-largest-closing-of-parishes-in-the-country.html.

Kasper, Walter. "The Ecumenical Movement in the 21st Century." November 18, 2005, online: http://www.oikoumene.org/en/resources/documents/commissions/jwg-rcc-wcc/the-ecumenical-movement-in-the-21st-century.

Kelly, Geffrey B. "Futurists and Reformers: The Shape of Tomorrow's Church." In *Theology Confronts a Changing World: The Annual Publication of the College Theology Society*, edited by Thomas M. McFadden. West Mystic, CT: Twenty-Third Publications, 1977.

———. *Karl Rahner: Theologian of the Graced Search for Meaning*. Minneapolis: Augsburg Fortress, 1992.

Kelly, Geffrey B., and F. Burton Nelson. *The Cost of Moral Leadership: The Spirituality of Dietrich Bonhoeffer*. Grand Rapids: Eerdmans, 2003.

Kenny, Mary. *Goodbye to Catholic Ireland*. Springfield, IL: Templegate, 2004.

Kenski, Gerhard. *The Religious Factor: A Sociological Study of Religion's Impact on Politics, Economics, and Family Life*. Garden City, NY: Doubleday, 1963.

Ludlow, Morwenna. Review of *Ordained Women in the Early Church: A Documentary History*, edited and translated by Kevin Madigan and Carolyn Osiek. *New Blackfriars* 90/1025 (2009) 131–35.

Bibliography

Mackay, Maria. "Church Unity Remains Top Priority for WCC." *Christian Today*, August 28, 2009, online: http://www.christiantoday.com/article/church.unity.remains.top.priority.for.wcc/24069.htm.

McCloskey, John. "State of the US Catholic Church at the Beginning of 2006." Online: http://www.catholicity.com/mccloskey/state-of-the-church-2006html. 2009.

Meehan, Bridget Mary. "The Case for Women Priests." Online: http://www.arcwp.org/art_case.html.

Meehan, Bridget Mary, Olivia Doko, and Victoria Rue. *A Brief Overview of Women Priests in the History of the Roman Catholic Church*. Online: http://www.romancatholicwomenpriests.org/RCWP_Resource.pdf.

Merton, Thomas. *Love and Living*. New York: Farrar, Straus and Giroux, 1979.

Metz, Johann Baptist. *The Emergent Church: The Future of Christianity in a Post Bourgeois World*. New York: Crossroad, 1981.

———. *Faith and the Future*. Maryknoll, NY: Orbis, 1995.

———. *Perspectives of a Political Ecclesiology*. New York: Herder, 1971.

Murray, John Courtney. *Bridging the Sacred and the Secular: Selected Writings of John Courtney Murray*. Washington, DC: Georgetown University Press, .

———. *The Problem of Religious Freedom*. Westminster, MD: Newman Press, 1965. See also, *Religious Liberty*. Westminster: John Knox Press, 1993.

Niebuhr, Reinhold. "Religion Fosters Social Criticism and Promotes Social Justice." In *Critical Issues in Modern Religion*, edited by Roger A. Johnson and Ernest Wallwork. Englewood Cliffs, NJ: Prentice-Hall, 1973.

Our Lady's Warriors. "Commentary on the Declaration of the Sacred Congregation for the Doctrine of the Faith on the Question of the Admission of Women to the Ministerial Priesthood." Online: http://www.ourladyswarriors.org/teach/inteinsi.htm. 5/29/09.

Radcliffe, Timothy. "The Shape of the Church to Come." *America*, April 13, 2009, online: http://americamagazine.org/issue/693/article/shape-church-come.

Rahner, Karl. *Christian at the Crossroads*. New York: Seabury, 1974.

———. *Foundations of Christian Faith: An Introduction to the Idea of Christianity*. New York: Seabury, 1978.

———. *The Shape of the Church to Come*. New York: Crossroad, 1983.

Rahner, Karl, with Karll-Heinz Weger. *Our Christian Faith: Answers for the Future*. New York: Crossroad, 1981.

Roberts, Tom. "Parish Closing Traumas Spread." *National Catholic Reporter*, January 23, 2009. Online: http://www.bishop-accountability.org/news2009/01_02/2009_01_23_Roberts_ParishClosing.htm.

Schillebeeckx, Edward. *Church: The Human Story of God*. Crossroad, 1990.

———. *The Church with a Human Face*. New York: Crossroad, 1985.

———. *Ministry, Leadership in the Community of Jesus Christ*. Crossroad, 1981.

Schmalz, Valerie. "Sex Abuse Claims Threaten Jesuit Universities." *Our Sunday Visitor*, March 4, 2009, online: http://webmail.aol.com/41757/aol/en-us/mail/Printmessage.aspx. 2009.

Shah, Anup. "Poverty Facts and Stats." Global Issues, online: http://www.globalissues.org/article/26/poverty-facts-and-stats. 2009.

Stammer, Larry B. "Attendance Is a Concern for Church." *Los Angeles Times*, April 10, 2005, online: http://articles.latimes.com/2005/apr/10/world/fg-decline10.

Steinhauer, Jennifer. "Film on Pedophile Priest Revives Focus on Cardinal." *New York Times*, October 7, 2006, online: http://www.nytimes.com/2006/10/07/us/07priest.html. 2009.

Stella, Tom. *The God Instinct*. Notre Dame, IN: Sorin, 2001.

Sobrino, John. *Witnesses to the Kingdom: The Martyrs of El Salvador and the Crucified Peoples*. Maryknoll, NY: Orbis, 2003.

Visser 't Hooft, Willem A. "Dietrich Bonhoeffer and the Self-Understanding of the Ecumenical Movement." *Ecumenical Review* 28/2 (1976) 198–203.

Weigel Gustav *Catholic Theology in Dialogue*. New York: Harper, 1961.

Wikipedia. "Catholic Sex Abuse Cases." Online: http://en.wikipedia.org/wiki/Catholic_sex_abuse_cases. 2009.

———. "Opus Dei." Online: http://en.wikipedia.org/wiki/Opus_Dei. 2009

———. "Óscar Romero." Online: http://en.wikipedia.org/wiki/%C3%93scar_Romero. 2009.

———. "Peace Corps." Online: http://en.wikipedia.org/wiki/Peace_Corps.

———. "Roman Catholicism in Spain." Online: http://en.wikipedia.org/wiki/Roman_Catholicism_in_Spain. 11/21/2009

Winfield, Nicole. "Italy Grapples with Priests' Sex Abuse." *Washington Post*, September 14, 2009.

World Bank. "Poverty Overview." Online: http://www.worldbank.org/en/topic/poverty/overview.

World Council of Churches. "JWG with the Roman Catholic Church." Online: http://www.oikoumene.org/en/what-we-do/jwg-with-roman-catholic-church. 2009

Essays from Rahner's *Theological Investigations*

Rahner, Karl. *Theological Investigations*. 23 vols. Baltimore: Helicon; New York: Crossroad, 1961–92.

Volume 2, *Man in the Church*: "Freedom in the Church." 89–107.
"The Dignity and Freedom of Man." 236–63.

Volume 6, *Concerning Vatican Council II*:
"The Theology of Freedom." 178–96.

Volume 7, *Further Theology of the Spiritual Life, 1*:
"Do Not Stifle the Spirit." 72–87.

Volume 10, *Writings of 1965–67 1*:
"The New Image of the Church." 3–29.

Volume 11, *Confrontations 1*:
"The Future of Theology." 137–146.
"On the Theology of the Ecumenical Discussion." 24–67.

Bibliography

Volume 12, *Confrontations 2*:
    "The Question of the Future." 181–201.
    "Perspectives for the Future of the Church." 202–17.
    "On the Structure of the People of the Church Today." 218–28.

Volume 13, *Theology, Anthropology, Christology*:
    "Possible Courses for the Theology of the Future." 32–60.
    "Experience of Self and Experience of God." 122–32.

Volume 14, *Ecclesiology, Questions in the Church, the Church in the World*:
    "Does the Church Offer Any Ultimate Certainties?" 47–65.
    "The Unreadiness of the Church's Members to Accept Poverty." 270–79.
    "Basic Observations on the Subject of Changeable and Unchangeable Factors in the Church." 3–23.
    "The Church's Commission to Bring Salvation and the Humanization of the World." 295–313.
    "Some Problems in Contemporary Ecumenism." 245–53.
    "Ecumenical Theology in the Future." 254–69.

Volume 17, *Jesus, Man and the Church*:
    "Opposition in the Church." 127–38.
    "Transformations in the Church and Secular Society." 167–80.
    "The One Church and the Many Churches." 183–96.
    "Third Church." 215–27.
    "Jesus Christ and the Non-Christian Religions." 39–52.

Volume 20, *Concern for the Church*:
    "Women and the Priesthood." 35–47.
    "The Future of the Church and the Church of the Future." 103–14.
    "Structural Change in the Church of the Future." 115–32.

Volume 22, *Humane Society and the Church of Tomorrow*:
    "Perspectives for Pastoral Theology in the Future." 106–19.
    "What the Church Officially Teaches and What the People Actually Believe." 165–75.

www.ingramcontent.com/pod-product-compliance
Lightning Source LLC
Chambersburg PA
CBHW072153160426
43197CB00012B/2362